Omaha: America's Hometown

by

Scott Peck

TABLE OF CONTENTS

Introduction………………………………………………………………3

Chapter 1 - Omaha: First Page in the Story of the Old West…………...6

Chapter 2 - Civil Rights……………………………………………….15

Chapter 3 - Introduction: Omaha Arts, Paris of the Plains………………26

Chapter 4 – Innovation………………………………………………...42

Chapter 5 - Omaha: Mother of Hollywood......................................74

Chapter 6 – Sports……………………………………………...............88

Chapter 7 - Omaha: The Heart of American Power…………………...102

Chapter 8 – Odds and Ends……………………………………….......118

Introduction

So many great deeds are achieved on the basis of dreams. Sometimes, the dream is industrialization and new innovations. Sometimes it is great art or music. Then there is the dream of growing something from nothing. The dream to create a city up from a wind-blown prairie. Today, most people do not dream of getting rich by platting out a new city, but in the early 1800's in the United States, it was a bona fide get rich quick scheme. It would become one of the few times when someone else's dream was the catalyst for millions of other dreams.

Omaha, Nebraska and its close neighbors have been the fulfillment of many dreams. The start of the city fulfilled the dreams of one William Brown, the proprietor of the Lone Tree Ferry in the much older settlement of Council Bluffs, Iowa. As the city grew from Native American hunting grounds, the city spawned the start of many lives and traditions that came to be a part of American life. Omaha became a font of American culture. A place from where American culture was derived.

There are elements of American History that have happened everywhere this is not discounted, however, some of the very elements that set major event in motion and affected the history of the world as well as the United States started with a flutter of a butterfly on the banks of the Missouri River. From the War of 1812 to the American movie industry, Omaha has had its hand in most of the cultural concepts that make up contemporary American life.

The Omaha area has quietly been a part of America almost since the very beginning. Lewis and Clark traversed the area in search of the mythical Northwest Territory. While their efforts did not bear fruit, they were successful at rediscovering the Western part of the country and encountering dozens of new cultures that would soon live in an area claimed by the young Republic. The first encounters with some of these people groups would set a tone and a precedent for the manner in which they would be treated decades in the future.

The geography of the metro area and the position of the great cities of the East meant that Omaha would become a nexus for people that would pass through or live in the area before moving on to the great American West. Native Americans and later fur traders helped blaze the Great River Road that starts just west of Omaha. It was this road that would become the route to take Mormons, then gold miners, and countless wagon trains to Oregon territory. This movement of emigrants meant that incredible amounts of human talent would pass through and indeed remain in Omaha.

As the periods of human migration ended in the United States, Omaha remained a cultural leader. The city spawned industrial and commercial innovation. Something about the area helped create some of the greatest American entertainers and musicians. Great companies and their Innovations were developed and continue to flow from this quiet metropolis. It may be the people or it may be something in the water, regardless, this book was intended to tell part of the story of Omaha. Since much of what has happened in Omaha touches on the story of all Americans, this book will focus on the parts of the story that are important to all Americans, not just the minutiae and nostalgia that mean something only to those who live in Omaha, Nebraska.

The story of Omaha does not mean that important elements of history and culture did not happen elsewhere. Rather, so much of the initial activities that created a cultural icon began in Omaha and in nearby locations that the area has truly become the birthplace of modern American culture. As research was conducted for this project, I found it very difficult to find any history or reference that explained the modern cultural significance of past events. So much has happened in Omaha that the world has little knowledge and unfortunately, so many people in Omaha, Nebraska have never been told the significance of those historical concepts that are commonly known in the city.

As you read, you will find that the stories are split up in sections to highlight the areas of cultural relevance the stories are part of. You will find sections on the Arts and entertainment, Building of America, Businesses, Civil Rights, Food, General History, Innovation, and America as a Superpower. Finally, readers will read a section on Omaha position as the creator of the Hollywood film industry in the TV and Movie Section.

Arts and entertainment will highlight artistic and cultural pursuits that have touched America. Some Omaha actions have created entire lifestyle choices and subcultures. Other artistic achievements have created amazing musical masterpieces that have become part of the mythical soundtrack of some of our childhoods. Historic Icons were products of Omaha and the area has a connection in the most duplicated artwork in world history.

Omaha, Nebraska has been integral in building America. Starting in the 1840's, the Gateway to the West started in the Omaha area. It makes sense that because Omaha was a nexus in the concept of Manifest Destiny that it was from this community that many other communities would rise up. It is not just cities that Omaha helped to build, but the infrastructure that the nation now enjoys. The infrastructure that has allowed cities to grow from large cities into individual metropolises was borne via different interests. First, commercial interests drove the need for infrastructure, later it was the fear of war and the need to protect a vast nation that fueled the ribbons of highway and transportation mediums that created lacework across the United States.

The highways out of Omaha carried not only ideas and products but also ideas that would change the history of the United States. America was founded on the concept of natural rights, that all men have the right to life, liberty and the pursuit of happiness. For a great period of our history, the disagreement was about who met the measure of a human being? Civil rights is not something that is generally thought of as an Omaha institution but the concepts and activities that people think of when considering the civil rights era are a part of the story of Omaha.

The changes in America over time affected all parts of life. As our world changed, the pace of life accelerated and forced the mechanics of family life to transform with it. Changes in the way Americans eat is a hallmark in a changing society. As women left the home and became active members of the workforce, the days of making every meal from scratch disappeared. New foods were created to meet the growing needs of families who found themselves with a dearth of time in their day. These new creations made other ways of dining acceptable and have since created American institutions. Since these first innovations in pre-made food, Americans have continually sought more instant and quick made foods to meet their needs. Today, America is inundated with fast food and rapidly prepared products that we can simply "nuke," when we want a meal.

Foods are not the only innovations that flowed from Omaha. The city is home to several historic companies that have been trailblazers in their fields. Some companies created hair curlers and bobby pins, while other enhanced their own vacation destinations. The innovators who were involved with the area have gone on to help change the world in profound ways. Sometimes, area innovators helped light the flame for iconic companies to catch fire and create their own history. The Omaha metro was quietly in thick of it all.

Omaha has been the muse and for more than just business innovation, it has also led the way in Sports. Americans have long been enamored with professional wrestling and Omaha has been in the center of the revolution. Farmer Burns sat as the grandmaster of America's martial art and produced a lineage of champions. The city is the home of boxing champions and underdog stories that set records and remain inspirational to others. The city has produced stars in almost every sport and produced true –stories ready for Hollywood.

Hollywood is a creation of the Omaha-metro area. Omaha has produced some of the greatest actors in the history of TV and Film. The city has also provided talent for lesser roles and for the silver screen. Producers from Omaha have created television history and directors from the area have created world renowned icons that have spawned other aspects of American culture like the ubiquity of video games.

Entertainment and video games are luxury items for safe and wealthy nations. American safety has grown from our military power. The United States has grown power through circumstance and then later by effort. Much of that power grew from efforts out of the heartland by people seeking to do their part to win wars and save lives doing so. The fist of American firepower was launched from the Omaha area and the symbols remain today.

This book is non-fiction and the information herein is true, however it is meant more as entertainment rather than reference material. Like so much of American History, the history of Omaha is often told without any interpretation or indication of further importance to the reader or student. This work intends to remedy this issue by explaining the historical record and explaining the significance to the reader. The intention in explaining the story of the area is meant to enlighten and catalyze further research.

1
Omaha: First Page of the Old West Story

When Omaha, Nebraska was platted out as a new city in 1854, it was one of the first cities west of the Missouri River. It was on the cusp of the frontier and was the interconnection of all the images that are conjured in the mind of what the Old West was and how it grew up. In the beginning, Omaha was complete with wagon trains and Calvary brigades setting out on the prairie. Fort Omaha would become the home of perhaps the greatest Indian fighter in American history, and in the same individual a General who had sentiment and understanding for his foe.

General Crook is cited by some as the reason George Armstrong Custer met his fate on an eastern Montana slope in 1876. It is hard to speculate what may have happened had Crook been able to join Custer that June afternoon. We do know that Crook's participation in the expedition with Custer, forever links him to the famous last stand and in the end, to Omaha, Nebraska.

In the early years, Omaha, Nebraska saw river boats move up and down the river. Gamblers and prospector passed through the city on their way West tom make quick fortunes at a card table or perhaps in some mountain creek bed. As the railroads headed west the Irish and Chinese laborers snaked their way from Omaha across Nebraska and into the great Western expanse. They followed paths that Natives had blazed millennia in the past and over which John Creighton had wired the country with the latest tech. The saloons and soiled doves followed the rails west from Omaha to gather their share of railroad money. Some would seek railroad gold by more nefarious methods.

In 1873 a Missouri gang travelled to Iowa with a plan. They would rob a train laden with Wyoming gold headed East for Chicago banks. The robbery was the first of its kind west of the Mississippi River and the execution of the crime was so audacious, the country took notice. It was the first major operation of Jesse James and the James-Younger Gang. Over the next few years the gang would become infamous for several robberies and murders throughout the Upper Midwest. Jesse James would become immortalized in Dime Store Novels as a kind of Robin Hood figure who robbed from the rich and gave to the poor. While the gang actually promoted this characterization on occasion, there is no verifiable proof of the gang actually giving money to anyone other than splitting it among members of the gang. The James gang did leave behind apocryphal legends all over the Midwest that they slept in innumerable family barns and makeshift hideouts while they were on the run.

One getaway that we know was true was Frank James marriage to Ann Ralston. The two eloped in 1875 and she was subsequently disowned by her father. It was short lived as she returned home with grandchildren when Frank James stood trial for his various crimes. James would live the rest of his life with Ann Ralston and go from outlaw to family man. Hanging up his formidable guns forever.

A man that may have been on the other side of the law but with the same legendary stature of the James Brothers was Virgil Earp. His early careers were varied and led him to travel throughout the Midwest. In the early to mid-1870's he frequented Omaha and Council Bluffs where he met the elfin, Alvira Sullivan in a café. He would be the only Earp brother to marry a woman who did not work as a prostitute, even if their marriage was only common-law. Virgil and

Allie would travel the country together as the Earp brothers followed one another to the opportunities the frontier offered.

In 1881, Virgil and his brothers Wyatt and Morgan Earp fought together at the OK Corral, perhaps the most famous gunfight in the Old West. Allie waited dutifully across town and helped nurse Virgil to health after he was injured by a bullet through the leg. She remained by his side his entire life. Virgil Earp returned to law enforcement throughout his life despite one arm being rendered useless in a failed attempt on his life. Most of the recollections of the OK Corral and the Earp brothers were gleaned from the mind of Alvira Sullivan, the sassy, Irish wife from Omaha, Nebraska forever links Omaha, to the events in Tombstone in 1881. That is why Omaha is America's Hometown.

By Hook or by Crook….Custer's Last Stand

Perhaps the most well-known event in the history of the west is that of Custer's Last Stand. It is the story of a glory hunting military leader who had made his entire career on daring deeds and sneak attacks, only to be massacred because of his own hubris. Or was it something else? Was Custer right in believing that he would be getting reinforcements?

In spring of 1876, the US Military launched a campaign against the plains Indians in order to drive them onto reservations. It became necessary to once again remove Native Americans from areas that had been previously negotiated by treaty. Prospectors found gold in the black hills in 1874 and almost overnight, what had been a small contingent of trespassers, passing for gold on Sioux lands, became 15,000 men all scrambling for claims and setting up mining camps.

It was the responsibility of the military to drive whites off Indian land but with this many it became a public relations nightmare for the army to do so. Newspaper editors consistently promoted the interests of the Europeans over the Indians and so the Army had little choice but to consider the relocation of the Indians. The Indians of course felt betrayed and many of them refused to even consider giving up the Black Hills which they viewed as sacred ground. Powerful leaders like Sitting Bull and Crazy Horse split away from the rest of the Sioux and worked to convince other tribes to join their struggle.

In early spring of 1876, Civil War Hero Philip Sheridan from his Chicago office set up a plan to subdue the plains Indians. He ordered a three pronged attack on the Sioux. He ordered Col. John Gibbon and his 6 companies to travel east from Ft. Ellis in Montana. He told General George Crook to travel north from Ft. Fetterman in Wyoming. The third prong was Brigadier General Alfred Terry's column moving from Ft. Abraham Lincoln in the Dakota Territory. Terry's command included the 7th Calvary under the command of Lt. Col. George Armstrong Custer.

The three armies were supposed to meet up near the Little Bighorn River in Southern Montana. The natives called the river the "greasy grass." Custer was in an incredible rush to reach the area and find the Indian encampment. So much so in fact that he turned down the opportunity to bring a detachment of Gatling Guns that were attached to his regiment as he believe they would slow his advance. Gen. Terry was aware of Custer's penchant for glory hunting and told him, " Don't be greedy, wait for us." Custer replied, "I will not!"

Custer pushed his men at a grueling pace, exhausting his troops. He was determined to find the Indian encampment first and find a way to defeat them quickly and gloriously. Custer's 718 troopers closed in on their quarry but Custer expected the other armies to show up right behind him and reinforce his gallant bravery. The other officers were dealing with their own challenges.

General George Crook had left Ft. Fetterman with about 1000 troops, 200 armed Indian scouts and dozens of armed civilians. Less than 30 miles from the meeting point he stopped his army to rest and have some coffee. They had no consideration that they might be attacked with such a large contingency.

As quickly as they stopped, a Sioux battle group fell on Crook's forces. The Sioux were uncharacteristically tenacious and willing to accept casualties. Crook's army fought a furious battle and were saved at least twice by their own Shoshone and Crow scouts. Crook's Indian scouts were excited to fight the Sioux who had attempted to destroy the respective tribes.

After the Sioux withdrew, Crook could claim victory. He had expended a great deal of ammunition and suffered several casualties. General Crook was apprehensive about pushing onward to the rendezvous and instead led his army back towards Sheridan, Wyoming where he waited for nearly two months for reinforcements to fill his ranks.

He was not in Montana 8 days after the Battle of the Rosebud when Custer fought 6000 Indians with 700 calvary. Crook was not available to assist Custer during his last stand. It is impossible to know if Crook's forces could have staved off certain defeat for the 7th Calvary though historians often argue this point ad-nauseum. There were myriads of things that could have been done to insure a better outcome for Custer and his men.

He could have rested them before the final battle. He could have accepted additional help from his commanding officer General Terry. He could have even used the Gatling Gun battery he had at his disposal. Instead, Custer attacked a superior force and died in glory.

General Crook would go on to a long career and become the most storied Indian Fighter in the US Army. He gained the respect of not only whites but also from his Native American opponents. They respected his blunt truths and total honesty. For his part, General Cook came to respect his adversaries as honorable and worthy men. The popular opinion about Native Americans soured badly after the Battle of the Little Bighorn. Americans who may have sympathized with the Indians were now decidedly against them and did not care about the injustices of forced removal. Just three years after the battle, General Crook was stationed in Omaha, Nebraska where he became one of the central figures in the greatest Indian rights case in history. It may be argued that this was one of the more important cases in the history of American civil rights as well.

Jesse James Slept Here…How Omaha Made Jesse Famous!

Omaha is often called the "Gate City," the opening to the Wild West. In the 1870's the frontier meant opportunity. Opportunity was a different concept to many. Some saw it as the opportunity to seek mineral wealth in the tributaries of California or in the mountains of Colorado. Others dreamt of building towns and building wealth selling lots and claims in the great American boom-town. Still others were altogether different. Misanthropic and bitter from experience in the Civil War, some veterans considered the wealth of the new nation surrounding them as a part of their severance or tribute from years in battle. One of these types was a man named Jesse James.

Jesse James fought for Missouri militias like Bill Quantrill's Raiders and the groups led by "Bloody Bill," Anderson. Near the end of Civil War hostilities, James saw many of his friends killed as the Union noose tightened around Missouri. He saw the dime store postcards of his friend Bill Anderson laid out in a coffin, his eyes fixed and dilated. Then in the closing weeks of th war, as Jesse James tried to surrender to Union troops, he was shot in the lungs. His wound, the death of his friends and the dehumanizing nature of war were all harbingers of his life to come.

After being nursed back to health, Jesse and his brother Frank immediately set about a career of robbery and mayhem. While the family James and their gang did gain fame for their deeds, they were hardly unique. The region and the time period were marked by general lawlessness.

Perhaps what brought Jesse James to the forefront was his connection to Omaha, Nebraska.

In July 1873, Jesse and his gang slipped into Iowa with dreams of a huge score. The Chicago, Rock Island, & Pacific had just completed their main rail line through Iowa and word reached the James brothers that $75,000 in newly mined Gold from Wyoming was on its way to Chicago. Jesse sent his brother Frank and gang member Cole Younger to Omaha to find out information in detail. The gang learned that the train was supposed to leave Council Bluffs, IA the third week of July and would pass by the newly formed town of Adair, Iowa on the evening of July 21st, 1873.

Jesse and the rest of the gang rode from Missouri to the hills surrounding Adair and set up camp. They set up their ambush on a lazy bend in the new rail line. They cut a notch in a hill that ran next to the rails. Jesse and the gang pulled up the spikes that held the rails to the track and tied a rope around the rail on the south side of the track and strung the rope up to the notch they had cut to hide in the hill.

In Council Bluffs, Iowa, Fireman Dennis Foley and engineer John Rafferty set off on their ill-fated final journey with two Pullman sleeper cars, four passenger cars and two freight cars in tow. They rumbled along the rails for the next 70 miles without incident. At about 5:30 p.m. on July 21, 1873, the engineer neared the lazy curve around the hill, the quarry entered the trap. The James gang pulled the rope and the rail pulled inward toward the other rail. Engineer Rafferty saw the rail suddenly move and took emergency action. He threw the engines into reverse but it was too late to change the fate of the train. As it reached the displaced track the locomotive lurched to the side and tumbled like a smoking giant onto the prairie.

John Rafferty was crushed under the hot, iron beast and died almost instantly. The boiler burst and belched pressurized steam onto fireman Dennis Foley. The dragon breath of the locomotive burned Foley from head to toe. Foley survived the initial wreck but succumbed to the agonizing injuries a short time later.

Like some sort of minor miracle, the Locomotive was the only part of the train that derailed. The rest of the train stayed intact and on the tracks. When the train suddenly stopped, the passengers were thrown from their seats and stunned by the calamity. None of the passengers were killed nor did any suffer more than minor injuries.

As the initial confusion wore off, the gang boarded the train guns drawn. They went straight for the express car which would have carried the safe and their intended target and forced the attendant to open the safe. Instead of the big score they had hoped for, the James gang found less than $2000 in paper money on board.

It was immediately obvious to Jesse and his fellow brigands that the intelligence they had gather had either been wrong or they had simply robbed the wrong train. Whatever the reason, the robbery was a failure in terms of the expected haul. The gang then returned to the passenger cars and deprived the stunned people of their valuables and cash. All the while yelling that they robbed from the wealthy and gave to the poor, a particular erroneous chestnut that would be repeated in dime novels and movies made about Jesse James and his gang over the next century.

Within 15 minutes and after collecting all the currency they could muster, the seven member gang mounted their horses and headed South. A railroad employee in the nearby town of Adair was alerted to the robbery and walked to the telegraph office in the neighboring town of Casey, IA and raised the alarm in Des Moines and Council Bluffs. Special trains were hastily arranged and hustled out of town to assist the stranded passengers and to begin the search for the marauders.

Men on horses tracked the path of the horses to the Missouri border. The railroad immediately offered up a $5000 reward for the capture of the perpetrators. As the posse organized by the railroads traced the steps of the robbers, it became clear that it was the notorious James gang who pulled off the first train robbery West of the Mississippi River.

There are differing opinions as to how the James Gang managed to rob the wrong train. Some say Frank James was identified in Omaha and his presence was deemed suspicious. To allay fears, the railroad decided to delay the train carrying the gold from the Wyoming. Still others believe that the James brothers simply got the wrong information and the real train passed by the same location of the robbery a day later. In the end, Jesse James and Brother Frank gained fame throughout the United States and the world through their bold but nefarious actions.

The robbery at Adair, while not the first train robbery, nor the first crime for the James gang struck a chord with the national and international media of the day. The mythical nature and romanticism that surrounded the James brothers created a variety of Old west clichés that exist to the modern day. The fateful train that made the James gang famous steamed out of the station on the South side of Council Bluffs, and it was from the Council Bluffs yards that men streamed to the crash site to pursue the malefactors.

Although it seems Jesse James legendarily slept in every other community in the upper Midwest, there is no evidence that Jesse ever spent a single evening in Omaha. It is undeniable that Jesse and his gang are inextricably linked to Omaha…Just another reason why Omaha is America's Hometown.

Heroes and Outlaws: Love in the Old West

The American concept of the Old West is often a series of different ideas gleaned from Dime Novels and the imagination of Hollywood Screenwriters. Most visions of love in the Old West are limited to soiled doves living in a saloon, cavorting with feathers in their hair and the quintessential dancing dress. The image of Miss Kitty pining for Marshall Dillon dances in the thoughts of many as TV and movies continue to re-enact the classic trope. Frontier love was often something different. Like so many other events, courtship and marriage connects Omaha to profound events in American history.

Alvira Packingham Sullivan was born in the community of Florence, Nebraska in 1851. Florence was developed as Cutler's Park by the Mormons in 1847 today it exists as a neighborhood on the extreme Northside of Omaha. The Sulivans moved seven miles south to Omaha when Allie was about 8 years old. This move brought about profound and tragic change in Alvira Sullivan's life. Within the next two years, her father would leave the family to fight for the Union in the Civil War. Within a year, her mother would take ill and die leaving 8 children alone in Omaha. The children were soon farmed out to various foster families. At 10 years old, Allie was acid tongued and pitiless in her honest opinions. This meant that life as a foster child was one of complete instability.

Allie Sullivan was shuffled from foster family to foster family as they grew weary of her opinionated and sassy personality. Allie was often fostered to families who kept her as a nanny for younger children. Her tenure with many families ended when they felt the urge to beat her or berate her with abandon. At almost all of the homes she lived in, she faced tedious manual labor and her own longing to see what was beyond the muddy, frontier village in which she was confined. Finally, she found refuge with her sister who was now living with a husband in Omaha. Now a teenager, Allie Sullivan found the opportunity to find her first paying job.

Allie went to work as a waitress in Omaha. She later moved to Council Bluffs where she claimed to have went to work at the Planters Restaurant in Council Bluffs, Iowa. It was here in 1871-2, that she first encountered the tall, wiry stagecoach driver as he sauntered into the dining room where she worked. The stage driver would later become town Marshall of Tombstone, Arizona, but on that day in 1871, he was simply Virgil Earp.

Allie commented years later that she remembered the moment the two met more clearly than any other memory in her life. Virgil Earp noticed her as well and was obviously smitten with the diminutive young Irish girl from Omaha. It was not long after that first meeting that the two were traveling together. For Allie to finally have a man who treated her kindly and helped her fulfill her desires to break out of the doldrums of Omaha and Council Bluffs of the 1870's and travel the country must have been miraculous.

Allie claimed later that the two were married in Omaha or Council Bluffs in 1874, but no evidence of legal union exists. Instead, despite the fact that Virgil Earp was married twice before meeting Allie Sullivan, the two remained together in sunshine and rain until the end of their lives. Whether common-law or legally wed, Allie was ostensibly with Virgil when he worked with more famous brother Wyatt as a Deputy Marshall in Wichita in the mid-1870's. She also claims that Virgil filled the same role with Wyatt in Dodge City, Kansas is 1876. While it is known that Virgil and Wyatt both resided in Dodge City at this time, claims that Virgil worked as a local gendarme are speculative at best and the actual facts are lost to the sands of time.

Virgil Earp and Allie Sullivan moved with Earp brothers, Wyatt and Morgan to Arizona Territory where in 1877, Virgil was deputized to assist the Yavapai Sherriff in taking down two area outlaws who were actively terrorizing the area. Perhaps the most fame for the Earps came in 1880 when the clan migrated to the aptly named, Tombstone, Arizona. Due to the recent murder of the town marshal, Virgil Earp was appointed acting Town Marshall. A year later, Virgil Earp would appoint his brothers Wyatt and Morgan as Special policeman and "Doc" Holliday as a temporary policeman in an effort to force a group of loosely confederated outlaws in perhaps the most famous shoot-out in the Old West, it became known as the Gunfight at the OK Corral.

After surviving the gunfight with only a gunshot wound to the leg that passed through the calf, the brothers faced a trial and Virgil slowly healed. Allie was nearly omnipresent by his side during this time. In December of 1881, one of the few moments that Allie was not with "Virge" as she called him, he was ambushed while walking down the streets of Tombstone. He was shot with a shotgun which struck him in his left arm. He would survive the attack but the gunshot rendered his arm useless for the remainder of his life. Soon after, Virgil and Allie left Tombstone to live near his parents in California. The couple stayed together until Virgil's death in 1905. Allie Sullivan outlived the entire clan who experienced the events of Tombstone, she passed in 1946 at the age of 96.

The Earp's were not the only couple who found frontier love in Omaha or Council Bluffs, heroes of the dime-store novel seemed to gravitate to the Omaha metro to find love or at least as an escape route to elope. It seems that even in the 1870's, some ladies fell for the rebel, bad-boys. It also seems as though Robert Burns was made correct when he proclaimed that the, "best laid plans of mice and men oft go awry."

Samuel Ralston was an Irish immigrant who immigrated to North Carolina and eventually became a wealthy planter and slaveholder. He moved his family to Northwest Missouri in 1842 and purchased an estate in Independence, MO. Samuel Houston was an ardent proponent of slavery and worked tirelessly to maintain slavery in Missouri and later to establish Kansas as a slave state. In Missouri he savagely opposed unionist Thomas Hart Benton and gave comfort to other Southern sympathizers.

This support of the Southern cause continued even into the Civil War. Ralston's land was the site of battled with the Union Army and elements of Missouri Rebel militias like Quantrill's Raiders and bands led by "Bloody Bill," Anderson. Ralston surreptitiously fed the rebel forces when they were near his farm, it is during these war time activities that he first met Jesse and Frank James. It may be during this time that Frank became acquainted with young Ann Ralston who would have been about 7 years old. After these activities were identified by the local union officers, they gave Ralston the opportunity at self-exile.

Ralston moved his family to Omaha, Nebraska and started a freighting business. His family developed friendships in Omaha and were well-known but his freighting business started to falter shortly after the war and he moved the family back to Independence, Missouri. Ann Ralston entered Independence Women's College and became a teacher. Where and when she met and became romantically involved with notorious outlaw Frank James is unknown. James recounted a story that he had bumped into her while she played croquet with a friend. That story however, is regarded as apocryphal.

It is speculated that their courtship was made possible through her first teaching job after college. She accepted a position in a small rural school just South of Kansas City allowing Frank James to visit without seeking her father's approval. It would hard to believe Samuel Ralston would have ever allowed such a relationship to happen had he known it was Frank James. James was an infamous man, 11 years older than Ann Ralston. Her father would have known him as a member of a murderous rebel militia. Ralston was notoriously protective of his oldest daughter's virtue prior to her marriage. Ann may simply have been wilier than her older sister.

In June 1874, Ann Ralston told her family she was heading to Kansas City and then to Omaha to visit friends and family. Shortly after, Ann was headed North with Frank James. She would be a June bride in Omaha, where she would also honeymoon on the banks of the Missouri River. Ann sent her family a note that indicated that she had married and was headed west. The truth came later when her brother uncovered the truth from one of the James' family. She had married Frank James! Ann was immediately disowned by her father but it did not seem to matter. Ann remained married to Frank James until his death in 1915. He was cremated and she kept his remains with her until she died in 1944, after which they were buried in the same plot to be together forever.

They say love conquers all, an adage as true today as in the era of the Old West. It might have happened anywhere in the country but for love, Omaha is forever wedded to the OK Corral and the infamous James gang. Just another reason Omaha is America's Hometown!

2
Introduction – Civil Rights

We often think of the Civil Rights era as a place and a time far away from Omaha, Nebraska. We remember the gritty black and white images of German Shepherds menacing teenagers and water cannons buffeting black people into a wall in some Southern town. The thought of the advent of Civil Rights being a product of Omaha, Nebraska rarely crosses our minds…but it should.

Cultures coming into conflict seems to be a mainstay in the history of Omaha. The city was planned and laid out by its founders while the land still belonged to the Omaha Indian tribe. The Omaha Indians signed it over as a hedge against their aggressive enemies, the Sioux Indians. The Omaha were cousins to another area tribe, the Ponca who in the 1870's were driven from their ancestral home along the Niobrara river in Northeast Nebraska and sent South to a place they did not know, to alive a life that was foreign in action and culture. When the son of Chief Standing Bear fell ill and on his deathbed asked to be buried in the land of his forefathers, it set forth events that would create the first real consideration of human rights that included people who were not White, Anglo-Saxon and Protestant.

Native Americans were the first groups to find a semblance of civil rights in Nebraska but theirs was not the only fight, nor were their leaders the only ones to emerge from Omaha redressing their grievances with a hostile majority. Malcolm Little was born in a small cabin on the side of a hill on the North Side. His family was harassed by "Night Riders," as a result of his father's fiery, black pride preaching. Malcolm would not live long in Omaha, but his time was poignant and marked his life. His life and religion became his signature as he fought for the rights of all African-Americans. He argued that his last name was the name of the slaver who owned his ancestors so he became known as Malcolm X.

While Malcolm was still embroiled in the enigma that was his early life, a Jesuit priest was sent to Omaha to work at Creighton University. It was here that he formed the DePorres Society and became dedicated to reducing racial inequality. Over a decade before the Sit-Ins were held in Greensboro, North Carolina, the DePorres Club staged successful Sit-Ins in Omaha, Nebraska. Before Montgomery, Alabama found fame with their successful Bus Boycott, the model for the even had been created in Omaha. The DePorres society was short-lived but has left a legacy of fighting for racial equality, not just for Omaha, but for the nation at large.

While Standing Bear helped bring attention to the plight of Native Americans, conditions overall remained roughly the same for many over the next 100 years. The frustration and pain of a century of disrespect and neglect came to a head when an Omaha native and dozens of other Native Americans landed on Alcatraz Island. Their mission was to reclaim the island that had recently been decommissioned as a prison and had become surplus government property. The idea was to create an Indian University and cultural center on the property that would help Native Americans find their way to self-respect. While the occupation was not a conventional success, the efforts of the occupiers were well documented on national network television and through occupation broadcasts from the island. The positive action influenced others and helped motivated the American Indian Movement to conduct further demonstrations for Native American rights.

While Omaha has certainly been a font of Civil Rights efforts, we have also dealt with struggles and tragedies. At the turn of the century, South Omaha was a haven for European immigrants of all types, In 1909, the haven became less than hospitable when a Greek immigrant was caught with an underage teenager. The man responded to the intrusion by shooting a police officer. The shooting caused a series of events that led to a riot. South Omaha residents actively pursued fleeing Greeks who eventually escaped into Council Bluffs, Iowa, effectively cleansing Omaha of Greek immigrants for a time.

In 1919, Omaha was faced with perhaps her most embarrassing nadir. After weeks of race baiting by area newspapers and the increase in African-American residents to the city during the "Great Migration," reports of black men accosting white girls became the concern of the day for the daily readers of the area newspapers.

On September 25th, 1919 a young, white woman, Agnes Loebeck alleged that she had been raped and named her rapist as a black man, Will Brown. With Will Brown in jail and the news media scourging his name in the dailies, he was already condemned in the court of public opinion. On the night of September 28th, a large mob met at the courthouse in downtown Omaha to bring about the actual death of Will Brown. The mob set the courthouse on fire and tried to kill the Mayor. In the end, the mob succeeded in murdering Will Brown. The mob raged for hours, finally posing for pictures with the charred husk of Willie Brown's body, perhaps the most infamous pictures of lynching in American history.

From tragedy to triumph, Omaha has been a part of all faces of the civil rights effort. It was where American Indians were declared human beings by a federal court and it was the place that became the catalyst for the greater civil rights movements throughout the United States. Omaha, cradle of American civil rights. Fitting for America's Hometown.

Standing Bear Proves He is a Man!

> Hath not a Jew eyes? Hath not a Jew hands, organs, dimensions, senses, affections, passions? fed with the same food, hurt with the same weapons, subject to the same diseases, healed by the same means, warmed and cooled by the same winter and summer, as a Christian is? If you prick us, do we not bleed? if you tickle us,
>
> do we not laugh? if you poison us, do we not die? and if you wrong us, shall we not revenge?

Perhaps it was sweet serendipity that the basic gist of Shylock's famous soliloquy was uttered in a Nebraska Courtroom by no less than an Indian. The powerful statement of those words changed the lives of Native Americans forever and returned a modicum of dignity to a conquered people. Perhaps not conquered by force of arms, but conquered by the precepts of Manifest Destiny. The Ponca people of Nebraska were certainly a product of the latter, but the words of Standing Bear unshackled his people to live as they pleased.

Standing Bear's people, the Ponca, like so many collateral people in the world, were the victims of politics and conflicts that had nothing to do with them or their lands. The problem for the Ponca began in 1866 when Sioux Chief Red Cloud led Sioux tribes, along with allies including the Northern Cheyenne and Arapaho tribes, against the United States government. The Sioux and its allies were seeking to protect hunting lands from encroaching settlers. The Americans soon found a tribal ally in the Crow Indian people. The Crow sided with the Americans for self-preservation as the lands that were being contested were historically Crow lands.

The Red Cloud War was essentially a type of Plains Indians World War. The Sioux and their allies had recently conquered the area seeking to take over traditional Crow hunting grounds, while the Crow and other tribes wanted to keep their lands. The Sioux found themselves fighting to hold the land they had won from other tribes as well as fighting the United States government who wanted to protect European miners who were traversing the area.

The Crow and the US Army fought from the three military outposts for three years. The Sioux and their allies made intermittent attacks with small forces meant to wear down the outposts. Occasionally, they would plan and launch major engagements. After struggling to subdue Red Cloud and his allies for three years, the US Army recognized that their efforts were unproductive and inordinately expensive. So in Spring of 1868 the government sent messengers of peace to the region and engaged the Indian leadership in treaty negotiations.

Red Cloud and the Sioux wanted the entire Powder River region which included the western portion. This meant negotiations with the Crow to buy their land and re-appropriate it to the Sioux. The Crow who had fought for the Americans out of self-preservation were betrayed on the end and forced out of their traditional land. Unfortunately, an error occurred in the negotiations and the Sioux were also granted lands in Northern Nebraska which included the land occupied by the Ponca.

In 1877, after prodding from the Sioux who had been the recognized owners of Ponca land since 1868, the government arrived in Ponca lands to quickly and forcibly relocate the people to Indian Country in modern day Oklahoma. This led to a forced march from Northern Nebraska to Northeast Oklahoma, a distance of over 600 miles. Nine Ponca people died along the way, including Chief Standing Bear's daughter which made the southward journey yet another Trail of Tears for the Ponca.

Upon arrival in Oklahoma, the Ponca depended on the kindness of other natives as they arrived to late in the season to grow crops. What the found there was a much warmer climate which infested the reservation with diseases. The Ponca were inundated with diseases like Malaria and Cholera which they had not faced when living in the Niobrara. Within 2 years, over 175 Ponca had died. When Standing Bear's son Bear Shield fell ill and it became clear death was imminent. He told his father that he wanted to be buried among his ancestors so he would not have to walk eternity alone. Standing Bear promised that he would return him to the Niobrara river of Nebraska. With two dozen followers, Standing Bear set out with the coffin of his dead son in tow. They set out on foot for Nebraska in January 1879.

After a tribe was relocated, it was a crime for the tribe to leave the reservation they had been granted. Knowing this, Standing Bear and his group avoided people and towns when they could, understanding that they may arouse concern in a large community and be returned to the reservation. They could not avoid the intermittent homesteads along the way but the white settlers tended to be sympathetic and assisted the group when they could. Standing Bear found his way into Nebraska and took his exhausted people to the Omaha Reservation to rest. The Omaha were distant relatives of the Ponca and so welcomed their old neighbors back to Nebraska.

Indian agents in Oklahoma had notified the Secretary of the Interior that Standing Bear left and in turn the Secretary notified Famed Indian Fighter General George Crook to arrest the wayward Indians. Crook, however, had different ideas. He had long since developed a sympathy and respect for the native peoples who had once been his enemy. Instead of arresting the Ponca expediently, he contacted newspaper editor Thomas Tibbles.

Crook knew Tibbles was sympathetic to the native cause and could publicize the efforts of the Ponca to return home. Public relations and sympathy would be sorely needed after the Massacre of the 7th Calvary had taken place just three years prior. Since that time, American sympathies for the "Noble Savages," had turned to antipathy.

Tibbles sent out daily reports on the efforts of Standing Bear and the tribulations faced by the tribe. The entire goal was to turn public opinion toward the benefit of the tribe. Crook did not stop with public opinion, he knew that Standing Bear would be called on the carpet in a court of law. He and Tibbles cajoled a local attorney named John L Webster to work on their case. He did the trial, pro bono as did another powerful attorney, Andrew J. Poppleton. Poppleton was the Attorney for the powerful Union Pacific railroad. His participation was somewhat surprising since the Sioux attacked a train near Lexington, NE in 1868 which helped lead to the Sioux ironically gaining possession of Ponca lands.

With legal team in hand and the newspaper working public opinion, Standing Bear, speaking for the Ponca sued for a Writ of Habeas Corpus in the US District Court of Omaha, NE. A writ of habeas corpus is a legal term that says that a person that has been detained or is incarcerated in some way can pursue a legal resolution that explains why they are being held or if the imprisonment is legal at all. This would mean that General Crook, the man who started off the issue to assist the Ponca would be made out to be the person who wronged them. Crook agreed if it meant the end result meant the Ponca were treated fairly.

In 1866, famed African-American abolitionist noted that the United States Constitution "knows no distinction between citizens on account of color." In 1879, Indians were not considered citizens of the United States, so Standing Bear could not act as a citizen of the United States. The removal documents that sent the Ponca to Oklahoma said that the Indians were wards of the

United States government. That the government controlled their fate. This was important because just 19 years earlier the US courts decided that Dred Scott was a slave and that nothing in the constitution could change his status from chattel to a citizen.

The challenge for Standing Bear was that he must cease to be a Ponca in order to be free. He was forced to renounce his nation which meant he and those who followed him to Niobrara would cease to be an Indian tribe and cease to receive assistance from the US. The second problem was that he was forced to prove that he was a man. That he could act as a man and think as a man. This idea was in doubt as many people of the time did not consider Indians "people," but rather something less than a human being, this was seen in when Standing Bear was first sworn In, the government Attorney objected, "Does this court think an Indian is a competent witness?" The Judge was forced to retort with language from the new 14th Amendment "the law makes no distinction on account of race, color, or previous condition."

In court, Standing Bear spoke through an interpreter and was defended by the aforementioned council. In the end, Standing Bear recognized that he needed to speak. "No man can speak for another as well as he can for himself," Chief Standing Bear explained to Thomas Tibbles. Tibbles arranged for Standing Bear to speak at the end of the Attorneys closing statements. When the time came, Standing Bear rose to his feet and walked toward the judge. He held his right arm out toward the judge and stated:

> "That hand is not the color of yours, but if I prick it, the blood will flow, and I shall feel pain. The blood is of the same color as yours. God made me, and I am a man. I never committed any crime. If I had, I would not stand here to make a defense. I would suffer the punishment and make no complaint."

He then spoke of his vision that he and his family was trapped between a violent, rising river and a man who was commanding soldiers. The man must make a decision to allow them to pass or let them be inundated by the water. Standing Bear pointed at the judges and stated, "You are that man." The judge sat with tears down his face. General Crook quickly covered his face and stood quickly to shake Standing Bear's hand as he sat down.

A few days later, Judge Elmer Dundy made his decision that an Indian was a man and that he was protected by inalienable rights of life, liberty and the pursuit of happiness. The Ponca were free to go and live as they chose. They were no longer wards of the United States which means they had to fend for themselves, but they could go forth and live where they chose and in what manner they could live.

Standing Bear's struggle did not end with the trial. His trial however opened a new and far more effective battlefield for Native Americans. Instead of bows and repeating rifles, the fact that an Indian was declared a human being and had rights was revolutionary. It changed everything for all people who were not granted the same rights as all other Americans. While the change in hearts and minds of all Americans was slow, the precedent set in Omaha was a huge step for all people seeking redress from the government in regards to rights and treatment.

In 1884 the John Elk case reiterated that an Indian cannot be a US Citizen and a member of an Indian Tribe, The 1887 Dawes Act further required renunciation of a tribe to be a citizen. In 1901, the US granted citizenship to Indians in Oklahoma. In 1919, Indians who served in WWI were granted citizenship. In 1924, the US Government extended citizenship to all Native Americans, although some states imposed restrictions. In 1948, Arizona and New Mexico finally lifted restrictions on Native American voting rights. In 1965 the Voting rights act was enacted which ended all restrictions on the right to vote for any US Citizen.

Standing Bear knocked over the first domino of equality for Native Americans but like the Ponca trail of tears, the journey was long and beset with tribulations. Brave men from Omaha helped bring about equality for others, even when popular opinion was against them. That is what bravery is.

Kicking Jim Crow's Ass Out of Omaha

On December 1, 1955, Rosa Parks became the first well publicized African-American woman to refuse to give up her seat to a white man on a bus in Montgomery, Alabama. This event is largely considered the beginning of the civil rights era in the United States. It also launched the career of a religious leader as a powerful leader of the African-American community in the United States. Rev. Martin Luther King Jr. Effectively led the Africa-American community of Montgomery in a famous bus strike that was one of the first real achievements of the Civil Rights era. Or was it?

Without diminishing the accomplishments of Rev. King and the many activities dedicated to civil rights in the South. Another religious leader, a Catholic priest, 1022 Miles to the North-East of Montgomery in Omaha, NE, started his advocacy and open assault on racism in 1947.

Father John Markoe was a Jesuit priest who with the assistance of black leader and newspaper publisher Mildred Brown, helped found the DePorres Club. Saint Martin DePorres was a mixed raced priest from Peru, whose great works included bringing enemies together into friendship. It was perfect for the non-violent Catholic order dedicated to as Father Markoe delicately expressed it, "Kicking Jim Crow's Ass Out of Omaha."

Father John Markoe led an amazing life and perhaps the successes he enjoyed in his early life offered a pathway to face the challenges of seeking racial inequality in a time that it was not part of the national psyche. Markoe was a West Point Graduated who was friends with Dwight D. Eisenhower and played football against Knute Rockne.

His first real contact with African-Americans was as commander of an All-Black regiment during the Punitive Expedition on the Mexican Border with the United States. It was during his service that correspondence with his brother would lead him to the Catholic priesthood and to dedicating his life to the easing the plight of "Negroes in the United States."

A decade before the general public had heard about racial issues and efforts to bring about Social Justice for African Americans, John Markoe was working to organize the African American community of Omaha to do just that. In 1948, the club participated in its first "Sit-In," of a restaurant located inside the Douglas County Courthouse, members of the DePorres Club successfully remained in the restaurant until the owner agreed to serve Black customers. This was 12 years prior to the Greensboro, North Carolina Sit-Ins at Woolworth Stores which were unsuccessful and remained segregated until 1965.

Markoe was devoted to the concept of Social Justice and sought various ways to promote the African-American community in Omaha, NE. When Mildred Brown and Father Markoe reviewed the list of employers in Omaha in the late 1940's they recognized that there were over 96 employers that would not hire Black employees. They fought this through pickets, advertisements and boycotts of various products. One of their first boycott operations was the boycott of the Omaha and Council Bluffs Street Railway Company for their refusal to hire black drivers and their consistently terrible service to the Near North Side of Omaha where most African-Americans lived.

The Bus boycott in Omaha by the DePorres club started in 1949, 6 years before the famous Montgomery Alabama Boycott. The DePorres Boycott successfully led to the hiring of African-American Drivers in 1954. The Montgomery Boycot ended with a Federal Court Case that ended segregation practices on the routes. During the same years, the club led boycotts against the local Coca-Cola Bottler and Reed's Ice Cream. The DePorres Club was a true trailblazer when it came to demanding civil rights for African-Americans.

Father Markoe fought racism long before it got widespread publication or was even popular in the United States. He did not receive widespread support, he did not have celebrity benefactors, his efforts were focused on the perennially poor and nomadic DePorres Club. Through its zeal and tenacity it was able to realize true success and become the pioneer and blueprint for the more famous civil rights movements that took place years after the activities of the DePorres Club.

Markoe said racism was "God Damned," strong works from a priest but these were his true feelings and they did not soften as he grew older. In the mid 1960's he became revered by his fellow Jesuits as Racial and Social Justice became en vogue. In 1967, as he lay dying and watched as race riots gripped the nation, he admonished his fellow Jesuits to "never give an inch."

Omaha: Laboratory for the civil rights movement.

The Adventures of Johnny Lobo

In 1887 the United States government implemented the Dawes Act. It was the coup de grace in the lives of Native Americans, the final major seizure and reallocation of Indian lands. Land given to the Indians was resold as surplus to non-Indian owners and the total land holdings help by Indians fell to a third of the original agreements. The Dawes act also eliminated the traditional communal property that most Native Americans had used for millennia.

Senator Henry Teller, the leading proponent of the Dawes Act stated, "If I stand alone in the Senate, I want to put on the record my prophecy in this matter, that when 30 or 40 years shall have passed and these Indians shall have parted with their title, they will curse the hand that was raised professedly in their defense to secure this kind of legislation."

Teller was prescient in his thought. Native American life effectively collapsed and the Dawes Act is often considered the reason Native Americans have remained an underclass in modern America. Native American civil rights and property rights stagnated for the next 80 years. Civil Rights returned to the collective Native American consciousness in 1968 as American Indians built off the African-American civil rights movement. The American Indian Movement was formed in 1968 in order to combat some of the disenfranchisement and ill effects that long term government policy had caused for Native Americans. Ultimately, the movement was meant to give native people across the Americas and Canada the opportunity to improve their living conditions, seek solutions to Native American poverty, substandard housing, and police harassment.

organization was determined for America to know who they were as an organization and to bring light to their peril. The first major AIM demonstration took place in 1969, when a group of Native Americans steered boats into San Francisco bay and landed on Alcatraz Island, site of the infamous federal prison. AIM saw this as a perfect place to occupy because it was federal land ready for reclamation by American Indians. The main spokesman for the occupation was a Santee Sioux/Mexican born in Omaha, Nebraska named John Trudell. The group issued a formal proclamations:

Proclamation to the Great White Father and All His People

We, the native Americans, re-claim the land known as Alcatraz Island in the name of all American Indians by right of discovery.

We wish to be fair and honorable in our dealings with the Caucasian inhabitants of this land, and hereby offer the following treaty:

We will purchase said Alcatraz Island for twenty-four dollars ($24) in glass beads and red cloth, a precedent set by the white man's purchase of a similar island about 300 years ago. We know that $24 in trade goods for these 16 acres is more than was paid when Manhattan Island was sold, but we know that land values have risen over the years. Our offer of $1.24 per acre is greater than the 47¢ per acre that the white men are now paying the California Indians for their land. We will give to the inhabitants of this island a portion of that land for their own, to be held in trust by the American Indian Affairs [sic] and by the bureau of Caucasian Affairs to hold in perpetuity—for as long as the sun shall rise and the rivers go down to the sea. We will further guide the inhabitants in the proper way of living. We will offer them our religion, our education, our life-ways, in order to help them achieve our level of civilization and thus raise them and all their white brothers up from their savage and unhappy state. We offer this treaty in good faith and wish to be fair and honorable in our dealings with all white men.

We feel that this so-called Alcatraz Island is more than suitable for an Indian Reservation, as determined by the white man's own standards. By this we mean that this place resembles most Indian reservations in that:

1. It is isolated from modern facilities, and without adequate means of transportation.
2. It has no fresh running water.
3. It has inadequate sanitation facilities.
4. There are no oil or mineral rights.
5. There is no industry and so unemployment is very great.
6. There are no health care facilities.
7. The soil is rocky and non-productive; and the land does not support game.
8. There are no educational facilities.
9. The population has always exceeded the land base.
10. The population has always been held as prisoners and kept dependent upon others.

Further, it would be fitting and symbolic that ships from all over the world, entering the Golden Gate, would first see Indian land, and thus be reminded of the true history of this nation. This tiny island would be a symbol of the great lands once ruled by free and noble Indians.

The occupation of Alcatraz was perpetrated by the group which called itself, United Indians of All Tribes. Trudell joined the occupation shortly after it started and provided the voice for the organization through his abilities in radio broadcasting. He used the Berkeley College Station at night in order to broadcast "Radio Free Alcatraz." The broadcast was a discussion of Native American Rights and the myriad of reasons for the occupation of the prison. One of the major demands Trudell consistently stated was the interest of the Natives for Alcatraz to become a cultural center and a Native American University.

While the occupation of the island was intended to be symbolic and somewhat short-lived, it became clear to the organizers that with some support the demonstration could extend indefinitely. To this end over 100 occupiers extended their stay. The federal government for their part, insisted that the Indians leave the island without any of their stated demands being met.

The original native group started to dissipate over the next six months and were replaced by tribal members who were not a part of the original movement. Additionally, members of the hippie subculture who were common in San Francisco at the time, also began to take up residency on the island. These new elements caused the original message of the occupation to breakdown in 1970.

The government tried to handle the situation through attrition. The Nixon administration told all stakeholder agencies in Alcatraz to disregard the Native Americans and do nothing to try and extricate them from the island. The Native Americans enjoyed some popular support outside of the area and the government hoped to wait till this support grew stale before taking any action. To expedite the situation facing the occupiers, the government shut down electricity and ceased all fresh water to the island. It was not long before the group that was left on the island grew desperate for funds and started stripping the building on the island of copper wiring.

The patience of the American government finally came to an end when in January 1971, two oil tankers in San Francisco bay collided. While there was no culpability in the absence of signals or lights from Alcatraz, but the accident in the bay was a perfect excuse for the government to end the occupation. In June 1971, members of the FBI stormed the island and expelled all of the remaining occupiers. When the last boat left the island that day, the occupation was completely over.

While none of the demands that John Trudell broadcast from the island were met, the occupation brought a long lasting recognition of Native American issues and launched a civil rights organization that exists even to the present day. The American Indian Movement or "Red Power," as it was sometimes referred was successful in bringing light to Native American plight. As a result of the occupation and other demonstrations, the US government abandoned the policies of Tribal Termination ended and passed the Indian Self Determination and Education Assistance Act of 1975.

President Richard Nixon also returned the Blue Lake Area lands to the Taos Pueblo Indians and created a new Indian University would be formed in Davis California. Nixon also increased the budget of the Bureau of Indian Affairs by over 200% and doubled the budget for health care among Native Americans. The Office of Indian Water Rights was also created to insure quality potable water was available on all tribal lands.

In the end, the plight of Native Americans may have been improved in many ways, it was not ended. John Trudell continued his life as a Native American Activist, fighting for what he felt were natural rights. Trudell faced tragic pitfall when his family burned to death in a suspicious house fire. His story was commemorated in a song by Kris Kristofferson entitled, "Johnny Lobo." Aside from his activism, Trudell wrote poetry and released several music albums of Indian/Rock Fusion. John Trudell died on December 8th, 2015. In his final public statement he said:

"My ride showed up. Celebrate Life. Celebrate Love."

3
Introduction: Omaha Arts, Paris of the Plains.

Omaha started as a rough and tumble frontier town. It was not built as a reflection of Paris or some other great European capital. There are no Van Goghs, no Rembrandts, no Picassos who tried to capture the beauty and the style of life in Omaha. Omaha was not considered a bastion of great art or artists of any genre, although it should be.

Omaha and its neighbors have produced great artists. In fact, the art that has been produced by Omaha born people has become iconic in the minds of Americans. Although Michelangelo never wrought the image of the perfect man from an ashlar of marble here in Omaha, the city was home to Gutzon Borglum, a man who created a monolithic sculpture that is revered by all Americans. His tribute to the leadership of America in South Dakota's Black Hills has become as famous and revered as Lady Liberty in New York Harbor. Another area sculpture has deep connections to the most reproduced artwork in the history of mankind.

Grenville Dodge was the chief engineer on the transcontinental railroad. His prolific abilities and early business acumen made him a very wealthy man. With this great wealth, his family enjoyed the best in life and in death. Grenville Dodge died in January 1916 in death as in life, his wife followed him. Mrs. Ruth Anne Dodge followed him in death in September 1916, but before she died a series of dreams led her daughters to hire the best sculptor of the day to create a memorial. While creating the Dodge Memorial, he was also creating another great American landmark that when completed would be reproduced on the back of the most widely produced coin in the world.

Omaha has also helped inspire great music and created social subcultures. Paul Williams gave us the Rainbow Connection and created the musical merriment of Jim Henson's Muppets. Omaha rocked the world when Lloyd Ingle belted out a drunken version of "In the Garden of Eden," creating the first Heavy Metal Rock Band and inspiring Matt Groening and The Simpson's. Heavy Metal gave way to Hair Bands in the late 1980's and early 1990's and Omaha anted up with Erik Turner, the founder of MTV favorite, "Warrant."

Omaha inspired rock music, Christmas Music and even novelty music that helped launch the trucker craze of the 1970's. Omaha even developed its own musical sound in the 2000's as Conor Oberst and Bright Eyes sang out their emotions to a national audience. All of these musical artists may have never hit the radio had it not been for the innovation of Todd Storz and Top 40 Readio.

In the end, Omaha is a place that is perhaps not known for its connection to fine arts nor any of the Nine Greek muses. However, Omaha artists have blazed out their trail in the world and their works are as famous as any of the great European masters. Omaha's contribution to American Arts culture is unmistakable. It is another reason Omaha is America's Hometown!

Why All Indians Live in Teepees and Want to Kill the White Man

Publisher, Edward Rosewater used his Omaha Bee newspaper to promote any concept that he saw as a good idea or would lift up his adopted hometown. In 1898, Rosewater, along with financier Gurdon Wattles proposed and produced the Trans-Mississippi Exposition to promote the Western States to the rest of the world. Rosewater ever the Omaha promoter, also convinced the US Postmaster General to create a set of stamps for the exposition, thus giving Omaha its own postage stamp.

In 1897, during the planning of the Exposition, Rosewater conceived the idea of the Indian Congress. The congress was meant to be a glimpse into the culture and lifestyle of Native American tribes before natives disappeared forever. It turned the exposition into a sort of zoo meant to display an endangered species. In fact, Indians were an endangered species. The Dawes Act and Indian removal acts were steadily destroying Indian culture. Rosewater theorized that the exposition would be the last opportunity to see Indians.

The Indian Congress was envisioned as a scholarly and educational look at what at the time was a fading culture. Organizers soon began to market the event as a far different affair than that original plan. Edward Rosewater was the head of the promotions department for the Trans-Mississippi exposition and was able to garner national attention for the event. This is remarkable being as this event was being held as the Spanish-American War broke out. The Indian Congress was soon promoted with the added attraction of "Sham Battle." Today they would be called re-enactments and they were coupled with the addition of Buffalo Bill Cody's Wild West Show.

The sham battles were perhaps the biggest attraction of the exposition based on the increase in attendance during the Indian Congress compared to before it started. Visitors commented on how realistic the battles were as they watched natives act as though they were scalping white men or as they "burned them at the stake." Indians fell on cue as the smoke belched from the rifles and continued until the whites had completely annihilated the natives. The glorious victories came with thunderous applause.

The Wild West show continually galvanized onlookers that that the Indians were a violent and savage people and that the end of their culture was synonymous with modern progress. Buffalo Bill Cody actually said as much in his address that the white man had endured "the trials and tribulations that we had to encounter while paving the path for civilization and national prosperity."

Edward Rosewater's newspaper printed the sham battles were "most interesting act in the proceedings of the day," as it represented a "dying nation" giving honor to "the greatest civilization of the world's history" that was "just commencing to play its great part upon the stage of the universe."

The Indian Congress had started out as a grand idea that was meant as an honorable display of a culture that was seemingly fading away. Buffalo Bill's Wild West Show and the promotion of the sham battles made the Trans-Mississippi Exposition one of the most economically successful expositions of the era, but it set in stone the cultural precepts that America held about Native Americans and their culture. When a more accurate depiction of native life was presented in Buffalo, NY and elsewhere at the turn of the century, the general consensus was that they could not compare and were not as accurate as the Indian Congress in Omaha.

And so the depiction of Indians from the Trans-Mississippi Exposition, that of predominantly plains Indians using teepees and war bonnets. Ready to attack whites at any given moment due to their savage warrior culture, became preeminent and predominated American cultural psyche throughout much of the 20th Century.

Rosewater came to Omaha after delivering one of the most profound messages in our history, that all people must be free. He helped one of the most important presidents in US History "tweet" out his messages over the telegraph line. He came to Omaha and presented what we today may refer to as "fake news." Sensationalist news that promoted ethnocentrism and racial offensive that it created the prevailing cultural image of Indians depicted in media throughout much of the 20th Century.

The spectacle of the Indian Congress and the heroic plot of Buffalo Bill's Wild West show all culminated in Omaha to create a vision of the Old West that probably never existed. Rosewater's vision created an image of Native American's as a savage and malevolent culture. The "reality," that onlookers were offered at the Indian Congress was of Plains Indian tribes, who were warrior based tribes dedicated to fighting Americans. Even though the Omaha Indians built earth lodges and actually lived very close, the Indian Congress displayed primarily teepees…as if all Indians lived in teepees. This was the predominant view that Americans and all forms of media held about Native Americans throughout the 20th Century.

Where Angels and Lincoln Tread

People of the Victorian era were obsessed with death. The reasons are varied but it may have been because of how close to death they always seems to be. Life expectancy during the Victorian era was far less than it is today. With rudimentary medicine and doctors, hospitals were the last possible port in the storm. Most people that entered the hospital in the Victorian age expected to die. For this reason, most people died in their own home, where their family experienced each and every gruesome step their family member took to their ultimate demise.

Infant mortality was much higher, children often died of simple diseases that today we wouldn't even dream they would contract. With all this death, Victorians devised ways to cope with and accept the condition of death. Victorians devised grand overtures and dramatic scenes of death. They performed séances, which were rituals designed to communicate with the dead. They even designed elaborate funeral services and customs for dealing with death.

After death, relatives were often expected to wear black for extended periods in honor of the relative who passed. Windows were draped, doorbells were muffled and houses were meant to be devoid of any music. The atmosphere was meant to be a dour affair. Family portraits were often taken when a close relative died because at death the family would often take any sliver of memory of their loved ones. Lockets of hair from the deceased were women into bracelets or necklaces.

Funeral proceedings were a grand affair for Victorian Caskets were often ornate and completed with a window so that mourners could see their loved one's face until burial was completed. The bigger the procession the better for the Victorian family, turnout indicated the quantum of love that was held for this person. The lavish funeral rites continued to the cemetery where headstones became elaborate sculptures and mausoleums were designed for people who could afford them. Victorians lived their life with death always nearby, this was true also of the Victorians of Omaha.

In 1916, a 93 year old woman living in New York experienced a series of visions. Strange visions of standing on a rocky shore, while watching out through the mist a boat approached her. At the prow of the boat stood a beautiful young woman resembling an angel. The angel carried a bowl under one arm and extended the other towards the old woman, inviting her to drink water from the bowl. The angel spoke to the old woman, "Drink, I bring you a promise and a blessing."

Then, according to accounts later published by Mrs. Dodge's daughter, Anne, the angel spoke twice, saying: "Drink, I bring you both a promise and a blessing." The old woman, Ruth Anne Dodge, wife of Railroad Builder and Civil war hero, General Grenville M. Dodge, imparted the story to her daughters. She had the vision three times according to legend she chose to accept the angel's offer and drink from the vessel. Md. Dodge said she felt, "transformed into a new and glorious spiritual being… I drank of that wonderful water of life and it gave me immortality," she told her daughters. According to her daughters, Ruth Dodge died very soon after the third vision. In death, the Victorian customs of death took over. She died at a home in New York but was shipped back to Council Bluffs, IA, her adopted hometown for internment in the Dodge family mausoleum.

Her daughters sought to commission the elaborate and ornate memorial that would insure immortality for their mother. The sisters sought out Daniel Chester French, to do the work. He was one of the most renowned sculptors in the United States and was prolific in his work. His first major work was the Minute Man Statue at Concord, MA. He also completed works for Harvard, Columbia, and Gallaudet Universities. In 1914, he started work on his largest and most famous work. It was during a pause in this project that he accepted the Dodge proposal.

The sisters gave meticulous instructions, a beautiful young woman with angel's wings, standing on the prow of a boat. One arm clutching a water bowl, the other beckoning those who witnessed the angel. The sculpture was mounted on top of a stone water basin and a fountain of water flowed out of the bowl and into the pool.

Verses from the bible were included in the work:

"Blessed are the Pure of Heart, for they shall see God. " Matt. 5:8

"And he showed me a pure river of the water of life; clear and crystal, proceeding out of the throne of God and of the Lamb. " Rev. 22:1.

"Let him that is athirst come and whosoever will, let him take of the water of life freely. " Rev. 22:17

The sculpture was completed and set in place in Council Bluffs in 1919. It is interesting to note, that the Ruth Anne Dodge memorial in Council Bluffs was placed only a block or two from the place that traditional lore says Abraham Lincoln used as a lookout while visiting Council Bluffs in 1859. Many believe the Lincoln story is apocryphal, but the memorial does exist in the shadow of the bronze angel. The angel was French's his masterpiece. Daniel Chester French expressed his affinity for the memorial on numerous occasions throughout his life. It would not be his most famous. That was the work he took a break on to finish the Dodge work.

In 1914 he started to work on a colossal sculpture of our 16th President, Abraham Lincoln. He worked on the Dodge project and the Lincoln project during the same time. He finished the sculpture in 1920 and it was shipped to Washington DC where it was placed in position at the newly built Lincoln Memorial.

The Lincoln Memorial might possibly be Daniel Chester French's most famous work. It was his largest, and it holds the quiet title of the most reproduced piece of artwork in human history. Don't believe me? On the obverse side of every penny there is a picture of the Lincoln Memorial in Washington DC. If you look with a magnifying glass, Mr. Lincoln resides in our pockets. From 1959-2008, the US Mint has reproduced French's image 100's of billions of times. But French's favorite work was one that interrupted the seated Lincoln, the standing angel of Ruth Anne Dodge connects the two works forever

Rocks, Coffee and a Crazy Genius

As the Senator who had become the benefactor to Gutzon Borglums's "Great Collossus," neared hid impending death, he waxed, "A week after I am gone, they will start to forget me. A decade and most people of South Dakota will be unable to even recall my name." The one they would remember is the brash, egomaniacal genius who had come to South Dakota to carve out colossal statues of Washington, Jefferson, Lincoln, and Theodore Roosevelt.

Gutzon Borglum's final work would also be his defining work. What began as a tourist attraction dreamed up in the mind of a state historian has become a work of art known throughout the world. It is the quintessential piece of American art one that all American's recognize, even if they have never been to the monument. A mountain of granite, carved by dynamite, from the mind of a master.

Borglum was the son of a Danish-Mormon polygamist in Idaho. After marrying two sisters, Borglum's father moved the family to Omaha, Nebraska where polygamy was not only frowned upon, but also illegal. This particular concept is interesting since it was in nearby Council Bluffs, Iowa just 25 years previously, that polygamy was first openly practiced by the Latter Day Saints.

After long standing issues, Gutzon's father divorced his mother but stayed married to his aunt. In Omaha, Borglum became an apprentice in a metal shop and entered Creighton Preparatory School in Omaha, NE. By the time Borglum was 16 years old, he was fiercely independent and had begun a keen interest in artistic expression.

After studying sculpture with Auguste Rodin in France, Borglum returned to the United States and earnestly began his craft. He was an almost instant success. One of his first sculptures won the Gold Medal at the 1904 World's Fair in St. Louis. Then shortly after be completed a bust of Abraham Lincoln. Upon seeing the completed sculpture, Robert Lincoln, the son of the late President commented, "I never expected to see father again." A true testament to Borglum's powers in manipulating stone. The bust was soon purchased for the people of the United States and is displayed in the Capitol rotunda to this day.

Ironically, it was this sculpture that motivated another group to hire Borglum to sculpt their memorial. The Daughters of the Confederacy hired Borglum to sculpt a magnificent mountainside sculpture in Georgia. The original design had Gutzon Borglum carving Robert E. Lee's head in the hug quartz outcropping known as Stone Mountain, GA. This would never suit Borglum's growing ambition nor his mountain-sized ego. To remedy what he charged was "as impressive as a postage stamp on a bar door," Gutzon changed the design to include Robert E. Lee, Jefferson Davis and Stonewall Jackson all on Horseback.

It was at the Stone Mountain project where Gutzon Borglum's larger than life personality and his willingness to fight his principles tooth and nail that would become a trademark of working with him. He fought with the administrators of the project and finally resigned in rage, destroying his models and fleeing Georgia with a posse at his heels. While he was not able to complete this work and none of the work he was able to do remains of the project, Borglum was able to learn and develop the techniques needed to do large works. During his time at Stone Mountain, he began discussions with a South Dakota group who asked him to review their project. Borglum saw a chance in the South Dakota project for national glory, that the Stone Mountain project never offered and was fine with heading north with his family to take on a new project.

Work on Mt. Rushmore began on October 4th, 1927, two years before the beginning of the Great Depression. Work began with over four hundred miners, rock climbers, and men who had worked with dynamite in the past. These men climbed to the top of the mountain each day and were lowered down the sides on swings which allowed them to blast, chisel and drill into the mountain. Borglum would scramble around the mountain as well as a supervisor to make sure the best angles were being taken to insure the effect he wanted.

While Borglum estimated a 4 year project time, the monument actually took 14 years. This was important because the majority of the time the work was stalled because of bad weather or lack of funds. Borglum was often engaged in fundraising activities and cajoling the Senator from South Dakota Peter Norbeck into sponsoring yet another funding bill in congress.

Gutzon Borglum by this time had become almost tyrannical to all of those who worked with him. While he was respected for his work and abilities, people were often intimidated by him or were simply unwilling to accept his domineering personality. He was an egomanic with an ego as large as his sculptures, but still, there were some parts of them that remained human. It has been said that one day he found his work crews huddled together in a warm place as cold rains poured on the mountain. They were drinking coffee to keep warm. Borglum seemed to recognize the sense of this and ordered that coffee and donuts be brought to the mountain each day for a morning break. From this impromptu pot of coffee was born the coffee break that is now enjoyed throughout the United States.

Gutzon Borglum believed that bigger was better and that is certainly a piece of American Culture. The Omaha boy who grew up to create a sculpture that is larger than the pyramids in Egypt, more famous than Rodin's "Thinker, and an almost innate piece of the American psyche. In the process he helped America have a sense of wonder throughout the depression. Something to draw them together until WWII forced them to cooperate as one people. Borglum has said that he left three inches more on the rock faces than he thought was optimum. With granite eroding at 1 inch every 100,000 years, he surmised that the rock faces would not be perfected by nature for 300,000 years.

Omaha = Gotham City?

Omaha has its Jokers. It has its Penguins, at the Henry Doorly Zoo of course. If we look real hard we might even find a Robin or two around springtime. Batman has become very prominent in American culture. The comic was first produced by Bob Kane and Bill Finger for DC Comics in 1939 as part of the Detective Comics. By 1940, Batman had become so popular that DC launched Batman as its own solo comic.

What does this have to do with Omaha? During and after World War II, the editors felt that comic books should not delve into such serious issues as a vigilante that actually killed criminals. To make sure of this, they made sure that Batman never had a gun and didn't kill anyone. Storylines were really directed toward lighthearted childhood imagination rather than the dark and complex storylines that came later. Throughout the postwar period, Batman comics started to grow stale and sales flattened. In the 1960's DC decided to revive the superhero by giving responsibilities to a new writer who re-vamped Batman to a slightly older audience.

In the meantime, children of the Baby Boom became teenagers and television was seeking content to fill the needs of this massive market. In 1966, Omaha native Bill Dozier launched the Batman TV series. The television version was filled with campy storylines, humorous lines and an upbeat soundtrack. It was also the only comedy of the time not to have a laugh track. The campy and often ridiculous nature of the television series bled into the comic books as well making this television series influential to the Batman universe. Dozier was not only the Executive Producer of the series he also played a few bit roles as well as serving as narrator.

Dozier was not the only Omaha influence for the Batman series. Batman always had a cool car. In the television series, he has a one of a kind car. Famous car builder George Barris created the television version of the Batmoile using the 1955 Lincoln Futura concept car. It was the only one of its kind ever built. It was a futuristic vehicle that was used as a promotion for Ford in the Auto Show circuit. The designer was John Najjar, the child of Lebanese immigrants, raised in Omaha , NE. He went to work for Ford Motor Company and once told Henry Ford he would rather draw cars than build them. Ford obliged and set him on course in the new Ford Design Program. One of his designs became the Lincoln Futura, what you know as the Batmobile.

While Batman only lasted three seasons on ABC, it was not the last of Dozier's efforts to bring superheroes to life on the silver screen. Dozier also launched the career of Bruce Lee when he created his next program, "The Green Hornet." Bruce Lee's portrayal of "Kato," the sidekick of Britt Reid, was so popular that it created interest in martial arts in the United States in the late 1960's. After the show was cancelled, Lee started acting in feature length films with heavy Martial arts themes. In the process, he became a pop-culture icon.

So from the often maligned, silly television show of Bill Dozier blossomed the live action career of Batman, which flowed into "The Green Hornet," and the introduction of Bruce Lee to America. Lee showed Baby Boomer teens what karate was all about and created a demand to learn the practice. In a way, Batman is from Gotham…er..Omaha, America's Hometown.

How Omaha created the 1970's Trucker Craze and made Christmas Cool Again!

Entertainment was different back then. Way back in the 1970's, there was no cable TV, no Satellite, the rare home recording devices usually played Super 8. People were reduced to…parents, cover the ears of your children…3 network channels!!! Somehow we all survived and America thrived without so many programs to watch. It seemed in the absence of so many programs and reality TV opportunities, advertising was created that attracted the attention of the viewers.

It all started with a bakery. Yes….a bakery. You know, pies, sweet rolls, bread, hamburger buns. Metz Bakery Company had just started operations in Omaha and brought its famous "Old Home Brand" with it. They needed a great TV ad and a memorable jingle to make sure they stayed on top of the flour pile. Their White Knight came in the form of a small-town country boy from Iowa, name Bill Fries. Bill Fires found his way to Omaha and started creating advertisements for the famous Bozell and Jacobs.

Bill grew up in a small town named Audubon, Iowa, right along Interstate 80…remember that, it is important later. Fries grew up idolizing the truck drivers that came to eat at the local truck stop and ogle the beautiful waitress "Mavis Davis." It was these memories all wrapped into a catchy tune and poetic television enrichment that became the ad Metz Bakery was looking for.

Bill brought CW McCall a truck driver for Old Home Bread to life. This trucker hauled bread on I-80 in his Ten Ton Bread truck and often stopped at the Old Home Filler Up and Keep on Truckin Café for lunch. At the café, Mavis Davis the waitress would serve him a meal using Old Home Bread products like sandwich bread, hamburger buns or sweet rolls. An entire story complete with a flirty romance played out over the consumption of bread. The television audience went crazy for it and filled their shopping carts with Metz Bakery items. It was so popular, people often called their local television station to ask when the next air time would be so they could make sure they could watch the one minute spot. Music teachers wrote in to ask Bill Fries for the lyrics so they could teach their classes the jingle. Most importantly people bought the bread!

Bill Fries who created the advertising story and sang the song won the prestigious Clio award for his work and launched an icon. Fries using the name of his fictitious truck driver parlayed the success of the ad into a singing career. As CW McCall he released 8 albums with a variety of themes, however it seems the majority always had the element of truck driving culture that he disseminated through his music. One of his songs in particular, "Convoy," was produced into a major motion picture. The film was about the adventures of truck drivers who were being abused by various law enforcement authorities.

The song and the film were a part of the CB Radio fad that swept the nation in the mid to late 1970's and was also a part of America's fascination with the truck driving lifestyle. While Old Home Bread and CW McCall may have been the very beginning of this piece of Americana, it certainly wasn't the only thing Omaha imparted into the American psyche to help create the trucker and CB craze. Omaha also has a connection to the Burt Reynolds hit film "Smokey and the Bandit."

So how did this make Christmas Cool again? CW McCall never released a Christmas Album that I have ever heard of. But the early commercials and the original song had a co-writer. Chip Davis didn't have the truck driver shtick of Bill Fries but his creative ability at composition and arrangement is world renown. Shortly after writing the Metz Bakery Advertisements, Chip Davis, and Bill Fries produced the aforementioned McCall albums. In between these albums, Davis created a new band and a new manner of composing Christmas music.

The band was dubbed, "Mannheim Steamroller," and featured Davis' personal technique of musical fusion between modern and classical techniques. In 1984, the band released Manheim Steamroller Christmas which sold millions of copies and changed the way America listened to Christmas carols. Since Mannheim Steamroller started making music they have amassed 19 Gold Records and changed American life. They gave us Fresh Aire and made Christmas cool again!

Paul Williams Connection

It is sometimes amazingly innocent and quiet when a phenomena appears. It's like the tiny piece of sand in the oyster shell that becomes a precious pearl. In 1976 and 1977, the proverbial grain of sand entered the shell when Jim Henson set out to make "Emmett Otter's Jug Band Christmas." It was his first feature length film and one of the first ever to employ puppets as the primary entertainers in a film. The feature length film sets were meticulously detailed, 3-D landscapes another first for Henson. The film was made without a buyer, something that wasn't done then and it isn't done now. Henson simply wanted to make the movie and make it without the interference of a commissioner.

In making the film, Henson and company used a variety of different puppeteering techniques like hand puppets, bunraku, and radio controlled puppets. The undertaking was like self-instruction on how-to make a movie with puppets as the main characters. He used film techniques and sets that he never attempted before. Jim Henson and his team invested far more time and effort in this project than they ever had before. The production was complex, and Henson wanted to=he music to be superlative.

Paul Williams had been a guest on "The Muppet Show," just prior to producing the Christmas show. At the time, Williams was perhaps the most prolific songwriter of the era. William's agreed to create the music for Emmet Otter's Jug Band Christmas.

In the winter of 1977, Emmett Otter's Jug Band Christmas was completed and sold to HBO in the United States and CBC in Canada. It became an instant holiday hit. It was nominated for 4 Primetime Emmys and won a Cable ACE Award. HBO continued to make the production a staple of their holiday programming for several years. With all the success, the Christmas program had ulterior motives.

Paul Williams says that when Jim Henson asked him to write the songs for it, Henson explained that he was performing a "trial run" for a proposed Muppet movie. All of the extra work and all of the special activities they did to produce Emmett Otter's Jug Band Christmas was intended to test the abilities of the Henson Company to handle the work and achieve the techniques needed to produce a polished full-length feature. If it had not been for the Christmas Special, there may never have been the Muppet Film Dynasty that extends to today.

Paul William's was an integral part of Emmet Otter's Jug Band Christmas but it was just a minor part of his work during the era. If a soundtrack of America had been created during the 1970's on which music was selected from all genres and uses, Omaha, Nebraska born Paul Williams might be the primary composer. He was a hit maker for TV, film and recorded music, working for musicians of a variety of sounds. He is also an actor who has played in dozens of films and television programs.

Williams created the music that made 1970's band Three Dog Night a hit band. They sang an "Old Fashioned Love Song," and "The Family of Man," which emanated from the mind of Williams. He also helped create the phenomena of the brother-sister duo in The Carpenter's. They lamented about "Rainy Days and Mondays," and rejoiced with "We've Only Just Begun."

His music was also covered by and used by a variety of diverse bands including Elvis Presley, Frank Sinatra, Ella Fitzgerald, Ray Charles, David Bowie, Tony Bennett, Luther Vandross, Willie Nelson, REM, Anne Murray, Gladys Knight, Diana Ross, Diana Krall, Sarah

Vaughn, Sarah McLachlan, Jason Mraz, and The Dixie Chicks. Williams has even contributed compilations for the French Electro-Pop Group Daft Punk.

The Paul Williams musical footprint did not stop at film and recorded music. Some of his other works are played daily into syndication, sung in busses during school road trips and used as a kitschy reminder of bygone times. Paul Williams created the music and lyrics for several of the biggest television programs of the 1970's including the ear-worm theme of "The Love Boat," as well as music for the John Travolta TV Classic, "The Boy in the Plastic Bubble."

Recorded music was not his only venue. He also provided music for film. He earned an Oscar nomination for his acting performance and the music he produced for the film, "Bugsy Malone." He received another Oscar nomination for his work on the Cinderella Liberty song, "You're so Nice to be Around." He didn't have to wait long to finally win the Oscar, in 1976 he wrote the love ballad "Evergreen," for the film "A Star is Born, which won him Academy gold.

Paul Williams also acted in a variety of films including contributing to the 1970's Trucker/CB craze through his role as Little Enos Burdette in the Smokey and the Bandit films. Williams was a key actor in the original "Battle for the Planet of the Apes." He also acted in various television shows and movies spanning the 1970's into the 2000's. Perhaps his most lasting and iconic contribution was his hand in the creation of the Muppets as a viable entertainment franchise.

With the release of "Emmet Otter's Jug Band Christmas," Jim Henson and company were able to perfect their skills to a level where they could begin work on a Hollywood movie. In 1979, Henson and the Muppet family began work on "The Muppet Movie" their first family musical intended for theatrical release. Jim Henson tapped Paul Williams to write the music for the film. When the film was released in June of 1979 it was an undeniable hit. There was little doubt the music was a big part of the success of the film.

"Rainbow Connection," became the most memorable song from the film and earned Williams a Grammy for his work. The soundtrack for "The Muppet Movie," was a certified Gold Record further cementing it's greatness. The success of the movie and the soundtrack created an entire Muppet franchise in which Williams participated musically. The popularity of Jim Henson and the Muppets rose in tandem with Paul Williams. Williams did not disappoint Henson. Williams noted, "You want to hear the songs as we're writing them?' Jim replied, 'No. I'll hear them in the studio. I know I'm gonna love them."

He must have loved them, and they must have appealed to the Jim Henson family and their fans. When Jim Henson died suddenly in 1990, it was the Paul Williams songs that the world said goodbye with. From Emmet Otter's Jug Band Christmas, the song "When the River Meets the Sea," from The Muppet Movie, "I'm Going to go Back There Someday," and finally it was the Rainbow Connection.

From the mind of one genius from Omaha Nebraska, came the music of many a childhood and the music that carried another genius off to the afterlife. Omaha is part of the foundation of the Muppets and their music. Omaha is Paul's hometown and America's Hometown!

Heavy Metal Simpsons

At a glance, Omaha does not seem to exude the teenage rebellion, the poetic angst that describes the players in the music industry. Out of the shadows of tall insurance buildings and through the plaintive cacophony of cattle singing their final dirge, Omaha has produced a musical progeny to rival anywhere else.

Children of the 1990's all wanted some "Cherry Pie," as they watched model Bobbi Brown run amok in the heavily played MTV Music video. As Omaha-native Erik Turner riffed on the rhythm guitar. It was a high water mark of the hair band he founded in 1984.

In the 1990's and into the 2000's the entire country found out what an "Omaha Stylee," is when 311 announced that they were indeed from this state as they pounded out funk-rap style they are known for. They were the vanguard for the Omaha-sound that broke out during the early 2000's.

Conor Oberst and his various bands all delivered their mournful outlook on life. Oberst could be compared to Bob Dylan, if Bob Dylan was clinically depressed. Oberst redeemed his downer music in 2005 with a crowd pleaser, "First Day of My Life."Oberst was involved with or inspired multiple other bands that flowed out of Omaha in the early 2000's some of which are still active today. The bands did enjoy success, maybe they are not a household name throughout the United States but they did give Omaha their own sound!

Omaha has been the subject of many a song. Bob Seger told us what it was like to be an unknown when the lights weren't on the entertainer when he sang, "Turn the Page." We know there was some thought as he rolled down the long, lonesome highway just East of Omaha.

The Boss, Bruce Springsteen also found inspiration in the Heartland. He didn't sing directly of Omaha, instead producing a solo album entitled Nebraska. This spawned more Omaha culture as his song "Highway Patrolman," became the plotline for Sean Penn's film, "The Indian Runner," which was filmed in and around Omaha and Council Bluffs, IA.

Grand Funk Railroad regaled us of stories of excitable young women who wanted to "get it on."

Four young chiquitas in Omaha
Waitin' for the band to return from the show
Feelin' good, feelin' right, it's Saturday night
The hotel detective, he was outta sight
Now these fine ladies, they had a plan
They was out to meet the boys in the band
They said, come on dudes, let's get it on
And we proceeded to tear that hotel down

It became the best-selling song of 1973 and was named #99 in VH1's Greatest Hard Rock Songs.

Perhaps all of these Omaha Rock appearances pale in comparison to the contribution of Douglas Lloyd Ingle. Ingle was the organist, primary composer and lead vocalist for the late 1960's Heavy Metal Rock Band, Iron Butterfly, Iron Butterfly is considered one of the first Heavy Metal bands ever.

Omaha born Ingle learned the organ from his father and in 1968 wrote his magnum opus in the 17 Minute, "In-A-Gadda-Da-Vida." The name stemming from the fact that Ingle wrote the song after consuming a gallon of wine. The song name had been intended to be "In the Garden of Eden," but Doug Ingle could only mete out an inebriated slur so the name stuck.

The song was incredibly successful and became the first ever song to receive Platinum status from the RIAA. While Iron Butterfly was part of a new and important genre of Heavy Metal. A Genre that would very soon produce thousands of pretenders, they themselves never really made much noise on the music charts. They never stopped inspiring. From this one song they put "The Simpsons," on the Omaha culture tree.

Yep, "The Simpsons," the long running animated Fox program has been running for nearly 30 years. One of the 600 or so episodes aired in its seventh season entitled "Bart Sells His Soul." As the episode begins, Bart Simpson switches the Church Organist's sheet music with a new song using the original name of the Iron Butterfly hit, "In the Garden of Eden." After 17 minutes of an elderly organist frantically pounding the organ, Reverend Lovejoy discovers the sheet music and sees that it was written by I. Ron Butterfly. Finally the music stops and the aged organist collapses onto the instrument as Bart unleashes the trademark laugh of the yellow miscreant.

Are you a headbanger? Are you into emo? Omaha certainly lays its claim to the Omaha sound being somewhere in the middle. The Omaha contribution to Rock and Roll is clear….but it might just be cooler to be connected to the Simpsons!

The Omaha Raisins????

The 1980's were a surreal time for United States and Omaha, NE was in the middle of it all. Ronald Reagan was president, K-Cars were the pride of Chrysler, New Coke inflamed the nation and Max Headroom was there trying to sell it. Kids were clad in neon clothes and Hawaiian prints as Billy Joel battled Michael Jackson for the king of the radio. If you were watching TV in the 1980's you didn't avoid commercials. You saw each and every angle, spectacle and jingle that corporate America could muster.

Claymation was a favorite medium of the day. The animation medium was seen in several advertising campaigns of the day. Domino's Pizza had the "Noid," MTV used it for portions of their programming and Kentucky Fried Chicken had Claymation chickens acting out why you should be eating chickens rather than burgers. Perhaps the most famous and memorable of these types of advertisements featured a group pf classic R&B singing anthropomorphic raisins reminding viewers to eat more raisins. The California Raisins became one of the most popular advertisements in television history.

In a very short time in the late 1960's, Jimi Hendrix became an incredibly influential guitarist. Even today his name is mentioned in reverent tones among musicians. His ability to create new sounds and to deconstruct music in order to make his guitar the core of the musical sound was his legacy. Musicians continue to try and develop this type of sound. Hendrix was against the war in Vietnam and often played benefits that sought to end the fighting. Some of his most famous music included his experimental style which created sounds of war, screams and weapons of war.

The most famous example of Hendrix style is "Machine Gun," a song he played on his final studio album "Band of Gypsys." It was the first he had created after his original ban "The Experience," disbanded. Band of Gypsys included a drummer and singer named Buddy Miles, an Omaha born musician who had played professionally with dozens of bands. In the late 1960's he was working with Hendrix who produced music for Mile's Band "Electric Flag." Hendrix died less than 5 months after the demise of "Band of Gypsys."

After Hendrix, Miles played with a number of other musicians and bands throughout the 1970's and into the 1980's. In 1986, the California Raisin Advisory Board commissioned a new ad campaign which featured dancing raisins singing a Marvin Gaye classic, "I heard it Through the Grapevine." But who was singing? Marvin Gaye was tragically killed in 1984, so in 1986 it was Buddy Miles who lent his soulful voice to the desiccated grapes.

The popularity of the California Raisins ad campaign was astronomical. Licensing agreements were signed for all manner of merchandise from lunch boxes, posters, Halloween costumes and action figures. There were comic books created to further the fictitious R&B Band's adventures. Probably the most important thing to happen for the 1980's was the development of a video game for the Nintendo Entertainment System. Although the game was created, it was never released to the public. The release probably had less to do with the popularity of the raisins than the demise of the marketing concept.

The commercials and the production costs were exorbitantly expenses and cost double the profits that the Singing, Dancing Raisins had garnered for the producers involved with the California Raisin Advisory Board. The cost over-runs eventually killed the s campaign and the Advisory Board.

The Raisins survived in their own short-lived Saturday Morning cartoon. Buddy Miles remained the troubadour for the production when agreements allowed for the California Raisins to create two studio albums. While their music had modest success, people were happiest seeing them in animate programming. CBS produced two prime-time specials with different adventures. The final merchandise licenses expired in 1998 and the original California Raisins faded from sight.

Although there are no new programs or other productions in the works at this time for the Raisins, the California Raisins live on in several pop-culture references and appearances. Several television programs have featured the raisins and they continue to show up occasionally in print ads and packaging. Their animation was inventive. Human like fruits always seem to be a hit. However, the fruits would never have had a voice without one of Omaha, Nebraska's musical sons, Buddy Miles.

4
INTRO- Innovation

The world is constantly changing. Omaha, believe it or not, changes along with it. Regardless of the glacial pace things sometimes seem to move in Omaha, regardless of personal feelings of Omaha being provincial or staid in its position on progress, the city has been at the forefront of innovations that have changed America and indeed the world at large.

The theory of Omaha's non-existent accent is that because the city was where all regional accents funneled together and hundreds of nations of immigrants created a single amalgam that the Omaha accent, refined itself to an accent undiscernible to most Americans. In short, we never talked funny because all the voices that did talk funny came to Omaha and drowned each other out. An accent that everyone can understand makes Omaha a great place for communications, which the city set out to be early in its development.

John Creighton strung copper wires from wooden pole to wooden pole out over the vast grasslands of the Great American desert. For 60 years, the telegraph was the king of instant communications. Lee Deforest would usher in many new changes that brought about wireless communications. Deforest also developed sound technologies that made "talkies," and animation with sound possible. In fact the Walt Disney Company owes its early history to Deforest and indeed to other Omaha area talents.

Omaha has produced great auto designers who created iconic vehicles like the Lincoln Futura and the Ford Mustang. Believe it or not, great design is something Omaha has often provided to consumer products. Carl Renstrom became the king of beauty products having invented effective hair curlers for an attractive price and bobby pins that worked. Renstrom became wealthy with his designs and used it to recreate Acapulco, Mexico into his own resort image. Renstrom constructed the Villa Vera in Acapulco and the city quickly took hold of their opportunity to be the resort location to the Hollywood stars. Throughout the 40's, 50's and 60's the stars would flock to the resort city. This was a changing time in America as well.

In Omaha, the accelerating post-war lifestyle and consumer demand for almost everything put America to work. The baby boom induced women to look for faster ways to produce meals. Swanson & Sons helped them do that when they invented the TV Dinner and sold busy mothers more free time dished into an aluminum tin and covered in heavy foil. Con-Agra foods got in on the act by enlisting the name of food connoisseur Duncan Hines to sell the boxed cake mix and frosting kit they invented.

Some years prior a nomadic entrepreneur worked together on an ice cream novelty covered in chocolate. The nomadic entrepreneur was Russell Stover and the ice cream confection was the Eskimo Pie. Russel Stover went on to be a candy magnate with his wife's recipe. It all started right here in Omaha.

With more time available to them, housewives could shop for more of what the modern family demanded. In Omaha, 6 months out of the year, the public was subject to extreme weather. Snow and Cold prevail in the winter months blistering, uncomfortable heat in the summer. A serendipitous Omaha developer built one of the first shopping malls in history, allowing shoppers to avoid the elements and relax as they shopped.

Who would have thought that Omaha was the place that put Rock and Roll on top? Sure, Memphis had Elvis Presley and Detroit was the home of Motown. An Omaha innovator name Todd Storz made the new music palatable. Eminem describes the misappropriation of black music as what put Elvis Presley on top of the music world, a model he emulated. Todd Storz made it acceptable and gave it a name!

Music is great daily entertainment but a resort is needed for a true vacation. The Union Pacific helped develop a great American resort to please the masses when they built Sun Valley in Idaho. A ski resort in the Idaho Mountains boasted unspeakable beauty and winter sports. The railroad put their prodigious engineering talents to work and developed a way for visitors to enjoy as much fun as possible during their day on the slopes by implementing the ski lift.

Almost 600 miles away, straight South, another type of resort was being built. Originally developed in modern fashion with Mafia money, Las Vegas was at first an absolute bust. It was the rare man or woman who wanted to travel to the middle of the desert to gamble. With smooth marketing and further developments, the public found what would become sin city. It was an Omaha man that made gambling palatable and affordable to everyone. Jackie Gaughen invented the concept of value gambling which made small casinos across the country a possibility and gave them an opportunity at profitability against the larger resorts.

Most of these events happened after WWII as America entered the Cold War. While America had developed highways throughout the country, new ideas were divined from German autobahns. The Interstate Highway system was designed, approved, and built allowing Americans to move around the country with ease. The roads were designed to be a part of American defense as was the vision of President Dwight D. Eisenhower. To take on the task the thousands of miles of new roads coursing across the nation, the US government tapped an Omaha construction company. While this company was one of dozens to contract, they had proved themselves to be worth their weight in gold during WWII. Peter Kiewit and Sons built more miles of the interstate highway system than any other contractor and continue to be one of the largest construction companies in the world. They are part of the fabric of Omaha's history. Kiewit and all of the other innovators are part of what made Omaha, America's Hometown.

Flying High with John Najjar and the Tuskegee Airmen

During WWII, Americans came together, they gave of themselves for the benefit of the nation. Communities from all over the United States gave what they could. North Omaha, gave several of her sons. The African-American community exhibited their patriotism as several young men joined the Army Air Corp during the war to learn to fly airplanes. Only the most intelligent African-American students were selected and so mostly college educated boys were allowed to submit for training.

These recruits were trained at Tuskegee Army Air Field and educated at the famed Tuskegee Institute in Alabama. The vast majority of these trainees learned to fly fighters as escorts for bombing missions. Some of the Tuskegee Airmen learned to fly bombers or in roles within a bomber, however these men never served during WWII.

The Tuskegee Airmen became known as first class fighter escorts in Europe. For years the Air Force claimed that the Tuskegee Airmen had never lost an escorted plane in combat. While this claim has later been proven to be apocryphal, their record was exceptional. The Tuskegee Squadrons were known to mark their planes with a very distinctive color scheme. The airman would paint the tails of their plane bright red, along with the nose cone and stripes on the wings. They often also includes bright yellow stripes as a contrast to the red. These particular color schemes led the Tuskegee Airmen to be known as the "Redtails." While the airmen flew several planes during WWII, they became associated mostly with the P-51 Mustang airplane. This was the fastest single-engine propeller plane ever built.

With the futuristic look and flashy paint scheme of the Tuskegee Airmen, the P-51 became the muse for many futuristic and sporty designs after the war. Including one design which has become synonymous to Detroit Muscle cars and is part of the dream of every teenage boy at some point in their lives. In 1961, Omaha native John Najjar began work on a new sports car. Ford wanted to build a smaller sports car to, "fill demand for cars between a go-cart and the corvette." Najjar named his new car the Mustang after his favorite airplane, the P-51 Mustang.

The small, light design and robust engine made the Mustang a powerful but small car. It was based heavily on vehicles Ford had already built, taking most elements from the Ford Fairlane and Falcon models. When the Mustang I concept was road tested, it proved to be fast enough to be just off the mark of F1 race cars. Ford Management rushed production and the first Mustang rolled off the lines in April 1964. Enthusiasts have dubbed this the 1964 ½ model. The first versions had been seen throughout 1964 and even appeared in the 1964 James Bond feature, "Goldfinger."

Upon release, the Mustang became the biggest seller for Ford since the Model A. It excited youth across the country and was simply the right car at the right time. The Ford Mustang has grown and be changed over 5 Generations of styling and 50 years of racing through American imagination. In 2005, Ford re-designed the Mustang line and took the car back to the original Najjar cars of the 1960's. From the great Tuskegee Airmen of WWII and their famous painted P-51s, Americans still see their grandeur through John Najjar's design of the Mustang.

Life is a Highway

42nd St and Broadway in New York City commonly known as Times Square is a quintessential image for many people around the world as to what America looks like. The theatres, the spectacle of street buskers, and the scramble of cabs and tourists that never seem to cease offer an exciting, indelible image of what America has to offer. Rather than the definitive look of American life, it is rather like the superlative illumination of what is to come as people pass from coast to coast on the Lincoln Highway.

The Lincoln Highway was started in 1913 by a group of automobile enthusiasts. Their mission was to create a paved roadway running from the Atlantic Ocean to the Pacific Ocean. In the age of hard rubber tires without pneumatics or hydraulic suspensions, the Lincoln Highway was meant to be a "rock," highway to make travel relatively easy. The main proponent of the road, Carl G. Fisher, knew that the car would never take off with the general public until they had an easy way to get somewhere. Good roads at the time were few and far behind, paved with an amalgam of off materials from oiled dirt, to seashells, to cobblestones, all were given limited maintenance. None of the roads went very far, they were really just connectors for merchants and to assist in local trade. The rest of the roads were rural roads, primitive and with little upkeep.

When construction began, Fisher named the road after his personal hero, Abraham Lincoln. It made the road the first and largest memorial to the fallen hero in the United States at the time. Fisher constructed the road with donations primarily from Henry Joy, President of Packard and Frank Seiberling, President of the Goodyear Tire and Rubber Company became the largest benefactors and in earnest the two chose the route across the United States. Henry Joy sought the straightest route from coast to coast. The terminals became Times Square in New York City and Lincoln Park in San Francisco, CA, Hundreds of towns and municipalities along the route were considered, the leadership sent out representatives from the leading newspapers of the day to choose which towns to include. Omaha was on this list.

Donations continued throughout the project, coming in from Woodrow Wilson, Theodore Roosevelt, Thomas Edison and countless other dignitaries of the day. The road even benefitted from the donation of 14 cents from an Eskimo village in Alaska. With donations flowing in throughout America, it seemed fitting that as the road grew and expanded across the nation, that the road would connect Americans to a variety of locations important to the history of the United States.

The highway passed into Weehawken, NJ, a strategic location for George Washington's Spies during the Revolutionary war, it passed Hoboken, New Jersey, where Frank Sinatra would be born just 2 years after completion. The road passes the grandeur of Princeton University and the homelands of inventor Thomas Edison. You can roll over the Delaware River at Trenton and imagine the icy Christmas Eve crossing of George Washington to exact a sneak attack on drunk, sleepy German mercenaries to win the Battle of Trenton.

The lazy road through Pennsylvania consumes the Lancaster Turnpike and the ancestral lands of the Amish as well as mirroring the Chambersburg Pike, the road that carried the Union Armies to the fateful turning point of Gettysburg. It carries the driver across the Quaker State to the Steel City, Pittsburgh, PA and exits into Ohio. The road continues through the bucolic farms and small towns of Ohio and into Indiana. The Indiana road moves us into Elkhart Indiana which became the "RV Capital of the World," and passed football glory in Notre Dame University in South Bend.

The Lincoln highway in Illinois passes over the Dixie Highway and the route of the "Mother Road," Route 66. In continues through DeKalb, IL the hometown of supermodel Cindy Crawford and the invention of Barbed wire, a profound invention that changed how land was used in the United States forever. From DeKalb we find ourselves in Dixon, IL, hometown of the great Ronald Reagan, finally exiting Illinois into Clinton, IA.

The road connects to Cedar Rapids, IA, surprisingly home to the oldest Muslim Mosque in North America. Highway 30 glides into Tama and past the only Native American settlement in the United States created by the tribe's private purchase of the land they occupy. The Lincoln Highway turns into Lincolnway. It passes land-grant, Iowa State University, a key player in the Manhattan Project and home to the first digital computer. Out of Ames and into nearby Boone, IA you find the birthplace of Mamie Dodd Eisenhower who would connect to a major change in American transportation in years to come. The road continues through the rolling hills of Western Iowa and turns south into Council Bluffs, Iowa, an area steeped in history. The highway passes into Omaha and follows the great overland trails across the Western United States. The Overland trail blazed by the original fur traders, the same road was hardened by the Mormons in their trek to Zion. The Pony Express would speed along the same line for 18 months until Edward Creighton used the area to build his telegraph. He trail became the artery to fill the west with gold miners and settlers and finally the transcontinental railroad. The Lincoln Highway did not break the mold and followed closely with these trails.

As the Lincoln Highway, passes into the old West as it enters Wyoming. Cheyenne, named after the Indians of the area by Council Bluffs railroad builder Grenville Dodge. Then through the hills and mountains of Wyoming. The road spills into the Wasatch Basin of Salt Lake City, Utah passed the great temples of the Latter Day Saints and into Nevada. Across the sage grass plateaus leading up to the Sierra Nevada mountains. In Carson City it connects us to the great Comstock Lode and the famed gold and silver mines of Northern Nevada. A second route goes through the "Biggest Little City in the World," Reno, Nevada and around nearby Lake Tahoe.

In California we climb up into the mountains and into the tragically named Donner Pass and into Northern California. Through the pine forests and small towns of inland Northern California the road connects to Folsom, California, the home of the state prison where Johnny Cash recorded his groundbreaking live album. Into the California state capital Sacramento and finally into the Silicon Valley. The original road ends at Lincoln Park in San Francisco but has been altered and extended to go passed Fisherman's Wharf on the Bay and onward to the Golden Gate Bridge, yet another classic symbol of Americana.

You see, Omaha is connected coast to coast by a colossal main street. The stretch of Lincoln Highway in Omaha remains pristine and perhaps the best example of the original 3,389 mile road. It is a product of the shifting routes and improvements that were common over the early years of the road. In 1929, the Abraham Lincoln Memorial Bridge was completed over the Missouri river which shifted the route from downtown Omaha through Blair, NE. This limited use of the road and left it in extremely good condition for a 100 year old brick road. Today the highway section in Omaha is still paved with the original red brick and limited to vehicles of less than 6 tons to keep it from degrading.

It was the paved highway that led to further economic growth and the acceleration of American progress. The iconic snapshots of America in San Francisco and New York bookend the history and the people of America, and Omaha in the heartland is the curator of America's first true road. The first monument to Abraham Lincoln and the first artery where commerce could ostensibly flow from coast to coast by automobile. The Lincoln highway was an engineering marvel for its day and proved that America could be connected in an affordable way. While rudimentary by today's standards, the road would inspire and grow into something greater. It makes sense that Omaha's Main Street, also known as Dodge Street, crosses America's Hometown and across the country.

Colossus of Roads.

American's love the automobile. In fact there are about 270 Million automobiles registered in the United States today. This love affair would never have been viable without quality roads. Cars would have only been a quaint novelty if roads were not built for them to move around on. The first was the Lincoln Highway, a road that started modern American travel. The catalyst for better roads came when Dwight D. Eisenhower traversed the United States after WWI in a military convoy. His experiences inspired him to consider to something better…but what?

It took 62 days to travel along what was the Lincoln Highway in 1919. Many of the roads in the east were well built and smooth but once the caravan reached the sparsely populated western states, construction became rudimentary and primitive. The caravan was at the mercy of the weather and the topography. Trucks would become mired in the mud of a spring rain and dragged down by sand and ruts. There were sections of the road that were so bad, that the convoy could have been halted completely and disbanded.

Interestingly enough, Nebraska was the first real state to create a torturous situation for the convoy. Eisenhower commented, "In Nebraska, the first real sand was encountered." "Two days were lost in western part of this state due to bad, sandy roads." The one shining grace was the fact that the newly built Omaha Athletic Club allowed the officers, including Eisenhower to use the facilities.

The convoy struggled on through the west through various trials and tribulations. The arduous journey followed the route of the Mormons and the 49ers and the military recognized the necessity of good roads. In 1919, it was hard to say what those roads would look like.

Dwight D. Eisenhower was profoundly motivated toward the concept of American investment in a highway system. Eisenhower explained, "there was a great deal of sentiment for the improving of highways," and on that point, "the trip was an undoubted success."

While the trip pushed congress to act and work towards infrastructure in the United States, it would be decades until the modern highways would actually be built.

The experience was only a part of the puzzle. In 1933, just days after taking power, Adolf Hitler he set thousands of Germans to work building a new road…a new kind of road. Germany created the Autobahn, a four lane divided highway that was completely paved. It was used for motor vehicles only which allowed users to travel the country quickly and safely. By the time WWII broke out in 1939, Germany had completed over 2000 miles of the Autobahn. Contrary to popular belief, the Autobahn was not built for military use.

In 1941 the United States entered WWII and fought against Germany. After three years of horrific bloodshed the allies finally broke through the German military and put them on the run. Once reaching Germany, the long problem of dealing with primitive roads in the European countryside faded away, the American liberators crossed the Rhine River and pursuing the Germany army became an almost problem free endeavor as they moved from dirt and cobblestone roads to the modern German Autobahn.

On May 8th, 1945, the German command finally surrendered and ended hostilities in Europe. Supreme Alllied Commander Dwight D. Eisenhower entered Germany and immediately became the military leader of occupied Germany. One of the first actions Eisenhower took in Germany, was to commission an intensive study of the German autobahn. While the German road was mostly rural, it became clear based on American vehicle usage and ownership, any similar road would have to have roads that connected to cities as well. When Europe had been purged of the Nazi armies a specter still lingered.

Months later, Eisenhower left Germany and returned to the United Status. The allies partitioned Germany and the city of Berlin. The Potsdam Agreement put half of Europe under the influence and power of the Soviet Union.

Eisenhower would return to the United States later in 1945 and serve his country in a variety of ways over the next few years. In 1952, he was convinced to run for president. When Eisenhower took power the Cold War had already begun to rage. He was able to reach a cease-fire and end fighting in South Korea. He set out seeking to reduce tensions with the Soviet Union. The Soviet Union had just developed their own nuclear weapon and so it became clear that all nations must be diplomatic to avoid terrible war, but must also be pragmatic about how to plan in their own country.

Towards the end of his first term in office, Eisenhower pushed his plan, a plan conceived in his famous 1919 convoy across the Lincoln Highway. The plan he galvanized when he saw a prototype governing occupied Germany in 1945. Eisenhower pushed for the passage of the Federal Aid Highway Act an act that would build the modern Interstate System in the United States. The Act went through congress easily partially due to the fact that the Act included a defense contingent. The roads were also meant to facilitate the defense of the United States. In the mid-1950's this became paramount in almost everything the government did due to the coiled snake of communism that seemed ready to strike.

When the Act was passed in 1956, the US Government tapped several companies to build the new Interstate. One of those companies was well known to the federal government. A construction company from Omaha, Nebraska was integral in ending world war two. This company had expanded Ft. Lewis in Washington State. Kiewit also built military installations throughout the Western United States and most importantly, Kiewit erected the Martin Bomber Plant in Bellevue, NE. Martin Bomber was the plant that produced B-29 for the bombing of Japan that ended the war.

Kiewit had even deeper involvement in this act. During the war they built the Big Horn Mountain Coal Mine in Wyoming. The coal from this mine was used to forge the casings of the Atomic Bombs dropped on Nagasaki. As we recognized the power of Nuclear power, Kiewit was there to assist the United States in developing new nuclear technologies. To do this, Kiewit built the Gaseous Diffusion Plant in Portsmouth, Ohio. The new plant was built to produce Uranium-235 for military and civilian uses. All of these achievements made Kiewit well known and a contractor of choice for the US government.

The Highway Act put Kiewit to work all over the United States. In their home state of Nebraska, they completed the Interstate system along the ancient, "Great River Road," faster than was completed in any other state. Soon Kiewit was building sections of Interstate throughout the United States which included some of the most difficult road building projects in the system. Kiewit helped to complete the Virgin River Gorge in Arizona which was the most expensive piece of rural interstate in the project due to difficult conditions, it would not be completed until 1973.

Kiewit continued to receive commissions for the most difficult interstate projects in the United States. This gave Kiewit the experience to build roads through mountains and valleys. They even successfully tunneled under Chesapeake Bay for an interstate segment near Baltimore. In the end, Kiewit built more lane miles of the United States Interstate System than other contractor, earning the sobriquet Kiewit: The Colossus of Roads.

Kiewit has been a key player in building out energy infrastructure from coal and fossil fuel mining to offshore oil construction. Kiewit has built a variety of dams and tunnels throughout the United States that most will never consider. But the company is so prolific that if you fly on a plane sometime, chances are, you can thank Peter Kiewit and Company for building major airport components around the United States.

If you have ever watched New England Patriot Tom Brady play football under the lights at Gilette Stadium. Kiewit did that. If you watched the undefeated New England Patriots fall to the New York Giants at Super Bowl XLII at Cardinals Stadium in Phoenix. You saw the pinnacle of innovation and engineering with Kiewit's design and construction. Millions watched Barry Bonds hit the first "splash hit," into McCovey Cove, at Pac-Bell Park in 2000, McCovey Cove was a feature built by…you guessed it, Peter Kiewit Co.

Kiewit has added to campuses and hospitals all over the United States. They have been a player in creating what many believe is the best zoo in the United States. The buildings they create do not bear the Kiewit name, and when the cranes and hardhats disappear, the people who use the buildings forgot how they got there. When America needs to build something profound they call Omaha.

Peter Kiewit has built America. The Interstate system helped Americans move around the country. With interstate highways, people flowed into California and made it America's most populous state. The Interstate projected power and freedom ad we moved product to every sliver of land in the country. Kiewit helped us build power through building production and research facilities and truly helped build the framework for American exceptionalism. Peter Kiewit Colossus of ……everything????

Edward Creighton: Disruption, Abraham Lincoln and Donald Trump

Modern entrepreneurs always want to be "disruptive." Their goal is to become an impediment of so transformative that consumers change the way they do which will change the way America does business. The thought is, changing the way America does business changes where the money in America flows. Today it is Apple and Tesla making the waves. US Presidents don't just use and abuse e-mails but they use Twitter to deliver their messages.

The first smartphone was released in 2007 which allowed us all to contact each other individually wherever we are. Being able to contact people almost instantly in the United States is not a new idea, it was accomplished through the work of Omaha's own, Edward Creighton.

Creighton was the son of poor Irish immigrants who overcame the era of "Irish need not apply," and antipathy towards immigrants and worked his way into personal growth and achievement. As a young man, Creighton was a "cart boy", this was usually a young man with a wagon an small team of draft animals who would carry freight over distances. It was the truck driver of the 19th Century. Later Creighton gave up his freighting business and started to work on grading railroad lines and city streets. It was while grading a street in Springfield, Ohio in 1847 that he bumped into what would become his life's work. While working with the road crew he found some other Irishmen who were putting tall posts in the ground. Creighton inquired as to what they were doing and they explained to him the new invention of the telegraph. Soon after, Creighton became the contractor to build the telegraph wire across the United States.

He started by setting the poles from Toledo, Ohio to Chicago, Illinois. As the country grew west, Creighton extended the lines. He stretched the Western Union telegraph system south into Missouri and Arkansas. Nine years later, in 1856, Edward Creighton recognized that following the frontier meant prosperity and so he went to the edge of the frontier with his wife and his brother John Creighton. Omaha at the time had only been in existence for two years. Creighton was the first wealthy man to choose to live in Omaha and he was almost instantly the leading citizen in town since the moment he arrived.

Creighton set about different business ventures as soon as he arrived. One fortuitous event which grew Omaha exponentially was the discovery of gold at Pike's Peak, Colorado. Omaha was positioned to be a "jumping off" point for thousands of people. A jumping off place was where people would outfit themselves for a long journey to wherever they planned to go. The Creighton Brothers became the outfitters for these travelers. Creighton also built ventures in banking and in cattle ranching while in Nebraska.

From the beginnings of American history, if products needed to be moved or messages needed to be sent, they depended on human effort with the assistance of animal power. During the mid-19th Century, the United States was a huge, growing country. The land area itself was the third largest country on Earth with major settlement and growth on the East and West coasts. That means that while the East coast could communicate easily because they were wired with telegraph, the West coast was isolated and still betrothed to the classic overland system of message delivery.

The Pony Express is one of the legendary pieces of Old West history. The Pony Express worked as a relay to send important messages from St. Joseph, MO across the Western United States to California. It was express, so speed was one of the most important concerns. To achieve their goals, the company set up over 200 "relief stations," from Missouri to California with fresh ponies and new riders. The overhead was so high that the average American was not using this to send messages or birthday cards. The service typically delivered government communications, business documents and newspaper reports. The modern equivalent of this service would be something like Fed Ex. The cost is higher than the postal service, but it is much faster and delivered as fast as possible.

The Pony Express was twice as fast as its competitors most of whom were stagecoach companies or steamboats travelling around the Cape of Good Hope in South America. A stagecoach could make the trip in about 25 days. The Pony Express made their trips in an average of 10 days, a mind boggling speed for the time. The personal best for the company was in March 1861 with the election of Abraham Lincoln. The message left Missouri and made it to California in 7 days and 17 hours. Within a year, the industry of message delivery would be disrupted and changed forever.

In 1860, the US Congress Okayed a bill to subsidize the construction of telegraph line from Omaha to Sacramento. The project would include two teams who would race to Salt Lake City. The first team would start building from Sacramento and Edward Creighton and his team would stat from Omaha and build across country to Salt Lake City. This same type of arrangement would be set up two years later when two companies raced to the center when building the transcontinental railroad.

In a little over one year, Edward Creighton had placed 26,000 telegraph poles and over 1100 miles of telegraph line across the United States. With a telegram sent on completion that simply said, "Done," the ability to instantly communicate with the East Coast of the United States was born, and the Pony Express, a venture that holds almost mythical status in the history of the West, yet never turned a single profit in its 18 months of existence, was also DONE. The telegraph was the final nail in the coffin of the Pony Express after losing over $200,000. The company was shuttered two days after the completion of the line.

The telegraph became a profitable venture almost from the moment of completion. If you thought Donald Trump was the first President who was obsessed with sending messages out using new technology, you would be wrong by 150 years. From the moment a telegraph office was opened next to the White House, Abraham Lincoln was obsessed with the technology and spent hours hovering in the telegraph office, yearning for positive words from the battlefield. It allowed him to project his voice to generals in far flung areas as easy as if they were standing in the same room. The telegraph allowed him to speak directly to the Generals without any interference with the message. Much like our current President's use of Twitter to communicate to individuals and the public without the interference of third parties.

In 1863, after sending out thousands of telegrams, President Lincoln sent out perhaps his most important telegram. It fell to a young Jewish telegraph operator to tap out the message. Edward Rosewater cracked out 719 words in Old Morse code, these words were the Emancipation Proclamation and his transmission, freed African-Americans from servitude. While the United States was large and the people were spread from sea to shining sea, Lincoln used the technology that god hath wrought and used it to transcend his location in Washington DC and have his president felt anywhere in the country.

Edward Creighton made much of this possible and from Omaha he wired the entire country. His technology disrupted industry, tied the country together and allowed a president to bring together a broken country.

From Hair Curlers to Tropical Paradise

Pink Hair Curlers are an almost iconic figure of American life. Women used these cheap foam devices as part of their beauty regimen for decades and Tip Top Products was happy to supply them to America. Tip Top was the creation of Carl Renstrom. Renstrom was an entrepreneur who was continually looking for an opportunity. He was the child of Swedish immigrants to Omaha, NE. His father was very mechanically inclined and actually filed his own patents.

After graduating high school, Carl sought out a variety of different direct sales opportunities but continually searched for new business opportunities. At one point, during the Great Depression, Renstrom was selling ads for Church Bulletins when he met a man selling a type of liquid solder that he was dispensing from a can. Carl immediately sought to create a partnership with the man but was rebuffed. Instead, Renstrom used the mechanical skills inherited from his father and sought to re-create the product. He was successful in his attempt to create a workable product and packaged it in a squeezable tube rather than a can. The ease and convenience of his packaging was perhaps the more important innovation, something Carl would remember. Customers responded which put Renstrom on track in life.

Soon after the solder business, Renstrom's sister returned from a trip in Europe with a set of hair curlers that she was excited about. Carl again reviewed the product and felt that it was a poorly made product and felt that he could make a better curler. Again, Renstrom considered the packaging that served him well with the liquid solder. The original curler his sister had purchased were selling for about five cents per unit, Renstrom sold four of his improved design on a cardboard card for ten cents and American responded by making Renstrom a wealthy man. Renstrom continued to build on this success and by the time he sold the company in 1964, Tip Top products was producing over 650 hair and beauty products.

Renstrom sold out in 1964 with the intention to retire, but this is where the story begins. When Carl first went into production in 1936 he was lucky enough to find a vacant factory just North of downtown Omaha. It was perfect as it already had an assembly line. It was built as an assembly plant for Ford Model T cars and pickups. Many of us have heard of Henry Ford's innovation of the assembly line, we may not have known his other contribution to American culture. It started with a Model T pickup truck. Model T's used over 100 board feet of lumber for the lining of the truck bed. This created a lot of waste and unusable wood. So in order to capitalize on this waste product, Ford employed a chemist to turn the wood waste into pillow shaped blocks that were called "charcoal briquettes." Ford sold them to smokehouse and restaurants but soon they were producing more briquettes than were demanded. Ford bagged them and started selling them in Ford Dealerships.

Sales were slow for the first 20-25 years but after WWII and the growth of Suburban development, Americans fell in love with the Weber Grill and outdoor Barbecues. Today people use charcoal all over the United States and around the world, even on the beach in Alcapulco. This brings us back to Carl Renstrom. In 1944 the Mexican government finally built a modern highway from Mexico City to Acapulco. This made it a prime opportunity, the kind Carl Renstrom was known for, so in the 1950's he built a personal home on the cliffs overlooking the beach and surrounded it with several private villas. Renstrom had a sense of wanderlust so he had homes in several locations and traveled for much of the rest of his life. Instead of watching over the property he entrusted Teddy Stauffer, often referred to as "Mr. Acapulco." Stauffer was a property manager and the exotic and, at the time, exclusive location, made Acapulco the perfect place for the Hollywood elite to get away from the maddening crowds.

The Villa Vera became the favorite place for celebrities during the 1950's and 1960's. Elizabeth Taylor celebrated her third of many marriages here. Frank Sinatra made it one of his haunts and Lana Turner romped with mobsters in the tropical sun. It all started with pickup trucks and hair curlers.

Skilifts of Omaha and the demise of Hemingway

"He loved the warm sun of summer and the high mountain meadows, the trails through the timber and the sudden clear blue of the lakes. He loved the hills in the winter when the snow comes. Best of all he loved the fall ... the fall with the tawny and grey, the leaves yellow on the cottonwoods, leaves floating on the trout streams and above the hills the high blue windless skies. He loved to shoot, he loved to ride and he loved to fish."

Who could be more deeply poetic in simple sentences than Ernest Hemingway? His words an ode to his final home. It was not in Omaha, NE, but instead in Ketcham, ID. Hemingway was lured here by Union Pacific President Averell Harriman. Harriman invested Union Pacific funds in the creation of a new resort in Idaho called Sun Valley. Harriman became interested in the concept of a winter resort after watching the success of the 1932 Winter Olympics in Lake Placid, New York.

Harriman had been a lifelong skier and had toured most of the European mountain ranges in his youth. After taking over the Union Pacific railroad, he sought to create destinations that people throughout the country would want to visit for their entertainment. Harriman enlisted Austrian sportsman Count Felix Schaffgotsch to find such a location. In the winter of 1935, Count Schaffgotsch found the area that would become Sun Valley in south central Idaho, about 100 miles northeast of Boise.

"Among the many attractive spots I have visited, this [location] combines more delightful features than any place I have seen in the United States, Switzerland or Austria, for a winter sports resort, " Schoffgotsch wrote to Harriman.

After finding the location, Harriman hired a publicist to develop the resort and start marketing it to the public. The publicist dubbed the resort, "Sun Valley." For his part, Harriman invited Hollywood celebrities from Errol Flynn to Marilyn Monroe to visit the resort. Their presence brought paparazzi and good press relations which brought in the people.

Winter sports in the late 1930's were just beginning to find a consistent following in the United States. Getting up and down the mountain proved difficult and this limited the "fun," part of skiing for many people.

At the time, if you skied down the mountain, you were limited ad to how you got back up the mountain. You could use a rope-towing method or you might try "skinning," up the mountain. Skinning is when a type of covering is placed on the bottom of the ski to help the skier go uphill on skis or to reach more inaccessible areas. The sheath-like covering is traditionally made from seal skin using the natural abilities of seals to move on icy or slick surfaces. When moving forward, the hair lays flat and smooth allowing the skier to glide over the snow. When the skier slides backwards, the hairs stand up and stop the backward slide. Harriman knew that there was a better way and back at the Union Pacific headquarters in Omaha, he set his engineers to work on devising a new system.

The new plan for human transport came from loading produce, specifically bananas. A young structural engineer named Jim Curran had seen large volumes of bananas being loaded with a conveyor that used hooks. He wanted to adapt this idea to human transport by changing the hooks to chairs and like the hooks, be suspended by a wire or cable above the chairs. Basically a skier would sit down on the moving chair with skis carrying them back to the top of the mountain.

While there was some debate regarding the safety of such a contraption, the engineers chose to follow the path and began in earnest to construct the device.

Paxton Vierling Steel in Omaha began constructing the chairs for the lift. Once completed, the engineers emptied one of the railcar repair shops in downtown Omaha to begin testing. Once the mechanics of the system were perfected, speed of the system was the final consideration. But how to test a system meant to work in icy and snow conditions in Omaha, Nebraska in the middle of Summer?

There aren't any mountains in Omaha and there are very few hills that would simulate a place to ski, so the engineers improvised. First, they mounted the new chair to the side of a truck. Then they had to consider how fast it should travel for a person wearing skis on a slippery surface. Using roller skates, the men maneuvered into position as the truck rolled behind them to pick them up on the chair. After several trials with the makeshift apparatus, it was decided that the engineers thought 4-5 miles per hour was the most effective speed for the lift.

The new system was immediately installed at Sun Valley. It proved to offer greater comfort and better capacity than the rope tows and toboggan systems of the past. As skiers became used to the new system, it became a big hit and in 1939, the system was patented by the Union Pacific as the Aerial Ski Tramway. The system has undergone several changes over the years but exists as nearly the same invention enjoyed all over the world today for skiing and other recreational activities.

Sun Valley became to the resort to bolster the Union Pacific's passenger service. Sun Valley became Ernest Hemingway's final home when he moved there in 1939 at the urging of Averell Harriman. It would be here in 1939 that Hemingway would complete what many call his greatest work, *For Whom the Bell Tolls,* his epic novel about his exploits during the Spanish Civil War.

Hemingway became a part-time resident in Idaho from 1939 for the next 20 years. While Hemingway was always a wanderlust when writing, he did return to Sun Valley for extended periods. It was here in 1961, after suffering from two major accidents during an African safari and continuing to feel the effects of a lifetime of drinking, that Ernest Hemingway cleaned and loaded his favorite shotgun and took his own life.

Sun Valley was an inspiration out of Omaha. It became a winter resort to promote the Union Pacific and attracted luminaries of all types from around the globe. The modern chairlift invented to efficiently move people back to the top of the mountain was invented for Sun Valley in the dark, greasy roundhouse in downtown Omaha, has moved developing skiers up the side of Round Mountain for decades. It helped create skiing champions like Picabo Street, and Snowboarder Kaitlyn Farrington. It was also inspiration to arguably the greatest writer in American history who finished his greatest work in Suite 206 of the Sun Valley Lodge. It was also where, after growing tired of the difficulties and pain of life, came to end it in the splendor and beauty of Idaho. The inspiration of Omaha the catalyst for it all and another reason that Omaha is America's Hometown.

Bombers, Brews, and Righteous Tunes...the Creation of Rock and Roll

A daily ritual of American life is to sprint to the car in the morning and the morning chirp of the dulcet tones of our favorite Dee Jay's voice. The zeitgeist of the day thumping from the stereo speakers. Our favorite songs bring us a euphoria as we weave in and out of traffic on our way to our jobs. We arrive at our desk and turn on the radio and not an hour later, that same hit makes the morning happy enough to read unpleasant emails from your boss. The dee jay comes on and makes sure that you know that he is playing 40 of your favorite hits. 40 Modern hits, it seems so right, so engineered. Was it always this way? From the advent of radio. God just gave us divine wisdom to recognize that we needed 40 Hits in a row and the best hits should be played several times per day.

Actually, it all started, as all stories do, with a great deal of beer. Gottlieb Storz emigrated from Germany to Omaha in the 1870's he went to work building a brewery and a beer empire that would last well into the 20th Century. When he died in 1939, Arthur Storz Sr. took over the business. Art was a bon vivant and something of an adrenaline junkie. He served his country in WWI and ruled his home and brewery with Military discipline. His affinity for the military and his top level connections helped him to attract top members of the military brass as well as war heroes and movie stars to his Omaha mansion. It was perhaps his influence and hospitality with Curtis LeMaywhich brough the Strategic Air Comand to Omaha and brought the cold war home to Omaha. The thousands of new airmen that came to Omaha would be thirsty for beer but something young men of the late 1940's and 1950's were really thirsting for was good tunes. Those would be provided by Art's brother Robert and his nephew Todd Storz.

While Art pumped out brews, Robert and Todd worked to pump out tunes. The two purchased KOWH radio from the Omaha World Herald newspaper. The purchase of the first station would be the first of several as the two formed the Storz Brodcasting Company. Storz Broadcasting Corporation purchased several stations throughout the United States and then went about changing the typical programming. The question was what would the new programming be? In the 1940's and 50's, radio was a mix of talk radio programs, some music and variety shows. In fact, most music on the radio into the 1940's was typically performed live. The recording industry in the United States really didn't get its footing and create a market until this time period.

Todd Storz began to study the industry and looked at the rating and number of listeners that each program of the day would receive. Storz found that when the stations played music there were far more listeners than when the station broadcasted a talk show. Once, Todd knew that music was the key to making the stations a bigger success, he turned the entire format to music, which included recorded radio jingles.

Radio Jingles were a way to brand one radio station in a market against another. Every station had one and they were each distinctive. It was usually music with the call letters and marketing slogan of the station sung by a chorus. A fictional movie example would be the most widely known. In the 1986 remake of "Little Shop of Horrors," a 1950's radio station had the upbeat jingle that went: W-S-K-D...SKID ROW RADIO!!!! These jingles were very memorable and continue even into the modern radio experience. This all began with Todd Storz experiment with programming.

Apart from adding the jingles, Storz looked at the musical format. He purchased a station that was using a Top 20 format and added an hour to the loop which added 20 songs. With this the Top 40 radio format was born. Storz was not finished with his experimentation with the invention of the Top 40. Legend has it that in a smoky barroom one evening, Todd watched people plug the jukebox and play their choices. As he sat and listened he noticed that these people were playing the same songs over and over. He realized that people wanted their hits. They wanted the favorites consistently and repeatedly. Storz immediately added this concept to his programming and the entire format was complete. Finally the most popular music was what the stations continued to feed their hungry listeners.

This was so much more important that it seems. America was at a crossroads at the time. Race was an incredibly important and very controversial topic. When black musicians created an R&B hit, music producers would rush out and find a white band that covered the same number. This meant that African-American artists were only selling to African-American audiences and stations. White audiences would be offered a white version. Controversial songs and artists drove away advertisers. With the Top 40 format, much of the racial struggle began to disintegrate.

Advertisers loved the new concept because they no longer had to worry about what new music would cause racial of social disorder. The most popular music is what played, that meant any music that was causing conflict or what receiving negative press was probably not going to make it into the Top 40. Rock and Roll went from a few black songs covered by white musicians to the preeminent form of popular music in America. The Top 40 format was the gateway for musicians of all races to find themselves on the airwaves. Rock and Roll was here to stay and Americans no longer had to consider the unsavory concepts of sexual deviance or the unthinkable at-the-time idea of miscegenation.

The honeymoon of limited controversy lasted for a time but the late 1950's is often also remembered for the "payola scandals," which led directly from the Top 40 programming structure...but that is another story.

The Top 40 format was the dominant format for 35 years until FM radio started to take over in the mid 1970's. FM had better sound quality and allowed for more stations in a given area allowing more stations to play to a varied audience. Top 40 is no longer what it once was but there is still a large audience who want to hear the popular hits of the day.

The Top 40 music format created dozens of stars that thrived on the programming. Dick Clark's American Bandstand and Casey Kasem's American Top 40 and dozens of other programs were successful because of Storz's invention. While Storz did not create the idea of Rock and Roll and he did not give birth to the sound, his incubation of the medium created strength and provided for it to grow and become the music of choice for the American public. For a time Todd Storz broke down some of the racial barriers of America. It helped dissolve some of the social morays of society and it created an iconic piece of American culture. It meant that the best music of the day was playing in Omaha, America's Hometown.

Life is like an....Eskimo Pie?

In 1994 a movie was released that connected with the American audience. Was it a drama? Was it a comedy? The film is hard to define but one line in the film sums up the entire crux of its message. "Life is like a box of chocolates....You never know what you are going to get." This line is from the blockbuster hit, "Forrest Gump." It was first uttered by the main character's mother, who was trying to describe to the mentally challenged "Forrest Gump," that life is usually full of the unexpected.

The 1920's were an unsure time for business and people. It was the early 1920's when an entrepreneur known for his wanderlust found his way into Omaha looking for a new opportunity. He had just cashed out his last endeavor, working to revive the long struggling Des Moines area candy confectioner, Irwin.

The Irwin Company was a setback for Stover but he and his wife were only in Omaha for a short time when a young soda jerk came to show Stover his new idea. The young man was Charles Nelson and he had just developed a treat he called the I-Scream-Bar. Stover recognized the opportunity but thought the name a gimmicky pun that would wear thin with customers. He change the name to Eskimo Pies and they were initially so popular that the men could not keep up with demand. It was the first time that chocolate covered ice cream had been sold this way in the United States. It was new and to this day, ice cream treats on a stick are referred to as a "novelty."

The new partnership was immediately beset with problems. Different companies were attacking the patent they held while others were simply selling their product as pirates and not paying for the patent. When a judge invalidated their patent a short time later, the two sold their respective shares to others and left the ice cream market altogether. Russell Stover and his wife took the nice return they made on the Eskimo Pie venture plus the $25000 they were able to sell their stake in the company for and it gave them the seed money to move to Denver, CO. It was in Denver that Ms. Stover started experimenting with making candy and developed Mrs. Stover's Bungalow Candies which became what is known today as Russell Stover's Candies.

Russel Stover's has packaged their candies a variety of different way since their beginning. One of the classic images of their chocolates in in a large rectangular box, hopefully with the flavors listed on the top cover of the box. This classic packaging is where the poignant imaging in Forrest Gump derived from. The slogan-like line from his mother was something he remembered and shared throughout his life. Russell Stover and his wive eventually moved their company and their production to Kansas City, MO where it remains to this day, but it all started with an Ice Cream treat in Omaha, Nebraska. A sweet reminder of Omaha's status as America's Hometown.

Let them eat cake....

Omaha loves to eat. The town was literally built to create food. From the stockyards and the influx of all manner of animals to the city grew legendary steak houses and restaurants. For decades, airports around the country had Omaha steaks pavilions for ordering cuts of beef delivered on demand. People in Omaha grew complacent that they always had something good to eat.

Until the advent of late-night diners or 24 Hour Taco Bell Restaurants, eating after hours was a tricky affair. So when men got the munchies while playing cards well into the evening during the 1920's, finding a bite to eat took creativity. In 1927, Austrian immigrant, Robert Schimmel owned the Blackstone Hotel in Downtown Omaha. Schimmel had a regular Poker night every Sunday at the hotel and all the players kicked in a little money to make sure they got a midnight snack from room service.

One night a local grocer, Reuben Kulakofsky ordered a corned beef and sauerkraut sandwich. The chef on duty was Bernard Schimmel, the owner's son, who strained the sauerkraut and mixed it with Thousand Island dressing. He stacked up the corned beef and topped it with a slice of Swiss cheese all on dark rye bread. He took the whole thing and pressed it on the grill, melting the cheese and crisping the bread. Reuben must have liked the sandwich and maybe Robert and the rest of the crew had a few bites. Whatever the outcome, Robert immediately put the new sandwich on the hotel's coffee shop menu and later he added it to the menus of his other hotels.

While his sandwich was famous regionally around his hotels it wasn't until 1956 when a waitress in one of the hotels entered the recipe into a contest and won. The Reuben has since spread across the country and found contenders to the throne as creators of a rather weird sandwich. So many people believe the sandwich came from one of the famous New York Delicatessens or from the mind of some long forgotten chef. Yet, the reality is it was created right here in Omaha when a bunch of guys had no fast food restaurant to stave off their playing card munchies.

It wasn't just late night snacking that needed to be conquered. When we get up in the morning we have to start the day off with a nutritious, well-balanced breakfast. Part of that breakfast might be an Omaha creation, Raisin Bran. Yes, Raisin Bran was invented by Lloyd Skinner in 1926. He was the first person to add fruit of any kind to cereal. It wasn't just fruit that he added to the cereal, he also added a small prize that made the cereal exciting for children. That made the cereal the first cereal meant to cater to children as well.

In 1944, the Supreme Court vacated Skinner's trademark of Raisin Bran as being to vague and only a description of what the product contained. This why we see several brands of nearly identical Raisin Bran Cereals marketed today.

The Skinner's at one time made pasta for sale all over the world. Another of their innovations included a fruit flavored powdered drink mix they called Quick-Ade all from their original downtown Omaha factory. Quick-Ade did not last and has been surpassed by its Nebraska cousin Kool-Aid but there is no doubt were the roots lie.

Of course, Breakfasts and Late-Night dinners all flow to one thing that everyone loves…dessert. Omaha has even created a dessert known all over the country. In 1952, a Con-Agra food chemist named Arlee Andre, developed a cake mix with great flavor that could be made by the average consumer. Andre developed a variety of different cake styles and formulated each mix. When the mixes were perfected and ready to be marketed to the rest of America, Con-Agra made like Nike shoes and got a celebrity endorsement. In the 1940's and 1950's, Duncan Hines, travelled the country and wrote books about his dining experiences. He created a rating system for Americans to plan their meals while on the road. His books on food and lodging became so popular that he began a syndicated column in the United States offering more frequent updates. In 1956, Con-Agra came up with a deal to pay him a penny per box to use his name on the new cake mix. The product became a hit among home-makers in the baby boom era. I guess Omaha just knows what tastes good.

Dinner in front of the Tube!

The end of WWII brought about great social change in America. It was a time when men were returning home from the war and the world was healing after years of trying to tear itself apart. It also sent women back to the home and back to the kitchen. In the coming years, Americans would start shopping like they had not done in decades. On their list of shopping items were the newest in technology, the tube television. Many people included televisions Americans would start families just after the war, bringing happiness after years of fear and dread.

With the growth of the family unit, and the time constraints that family life brings. Housewives and mothers started to search for foods that would give them more time.

Cooking is a time intensive process. You have to buy your ingredients, process those ingredients, and cook those foods into whatever dish you were planning. Foods like mashed potatoes and fried chicken were especially time consuming and making them meant you had less time to clean the house, feed the babies, and keep up with the laundry. All the duties of the 1950's housewife.

CJ Swanson and sons recognized a need in the market and went about fulfilling that need. CJ Swanson and Sons had already been in business for a number of years selling processed food to grocery stores. Their most successful early products were turkey and poultry sold in cans or sold frozen.

Legend has it, that after a bad 1952 Thanksgiving season, the Swanson brothers freezers were overstocked with 520,000 pounds of frozen turkey. Without a plan as to what to do with it all they were planning to store the meat in refrigerated railroad cars. The glut of meat gave them the opportunity to experiment with a new product. The product was the Swanson TV Brand Frozen Dinner. It included Turkey, Cornbread Stuffing, frozen peas, and mashed sweet potatoes all served in a compartmentalized aluminum tin with a sheet of aluminum foil sealing the top closed. Swanson produced the dinners at its factory in downtown Omaha, NE. The first year of production saw Swanson ship over 10 Million meals.

While frozen dinners had been sold elsewhere by different companies, perhaps the genius of TV Dinners was in the packaging. Consumers found that they didn't need anything else to cook with, no extra dishes or tools, and they could eat directly from the hot tin, resting on a TV tray while watching "The Honeymooners," or "I Love Lucy."

The aluminum tin may have even provided the name for the meals as well. This was the 1950's and TV technology was still brand new. A 12 inch screen was a "Big" screen. The tin resembled a television and the outer packaging of the meal often featured a television set. This time period also played on the new technologies that were happening elsewhere including space exploration. In short, the excitement around the TV dinner was as much about the futuristic look of the product and the futuristic zeitgeist that gripped America after WWII.

In the early days of the TV dinner, the meals were competing mostly with home cooked meals. Housewives used the meals as a way to save time or as a convenience. The fact that they served as their own dish meant that dinner could be served and the family could enjoy the new invention in the living room and nobody had to cut the evening short to wash a load of dishes. This was not universally accepted in America. Some men wanted their wives to be at home cooking all day like their mothers did. Convenience foods like TV dinners gave women more time to venture out into hobbies and even part-time jobs! Mon Dieu!! You could say that the TV

Dinner was one small step towards the women's liberation movement. Maybe you didn't hear Helen Reddy singing, but it was another step up the ladder of equality.

As society changed and the Baby Boom grew up in front of the TV. The meals changed to meet the needs of the changing society. Swanson added more sophisticated flavors and dinner options like the Polynesian Shrimp Dinner, German Style Meals like Sauerbraten and even a Mexican dinner which included tamales and Spanish rice. In the 1970's, Swanson recognized the needs of bigger appetites by launching the "Hungry Man" Dinners. Swanson enlisted a huge appetite by using Mean Joe Greene as a spokesperson for the Hungry Man dinner, further enlisting the feeling of the day as Mean Joe Greene played for the Super Bowl Champion Pittsburgh Steelers.

In the 1980's Swanson developed a plastic tray for microwave cooking. They no longer use a "futuristic," aluminum tin for their meals and Swanson dropped the TV Dinner name in 1962, but the name still rings and live on in the modern day. The future of the TV Dinner is in flux in the modern day. Swanson is a shadow of what it once was.

The factory in Omaha has been imploded making way for the Holland Performing Arts Center in Omaha but on the East end of the building once stood a building that fed millions of people and started to bring women out of the kitchen, giving them an opportunity to be mothers as well a enjoying other aspects of life. A pop culture icon was born all because of too many Thanksgiving turkeys in Omaha, NE. Icon? What else would you call something that has made its way into the Smithsonian in Washington DC. Not bad for the frozen food aisle!

Wanna Go the Mall?

The American retail industry has long sought out methods to separate we numerous fools from our money. From new products and packaging to different ways to buy to different ways to shop. Most Americans today grew up with the shopping mall. In cold weather areas a fully enclosed shopping center was a necessity. Malls eliminated outdoor walking and weathering the often artic like weather of cities like Omaha. The mall allowed you to park your car and enter the mellow warmth of the shopping center, allowing the shopper to shop in safety and peace.

Since the mall became ubiquitous in the United States, it has gone beyond a place of commerce and became a piece of American social culture.

The mall became a place for a subset of Young Americans to go to see and be seen. Magazines and movies have chronicled how teenagers have utilized the shopping mall as a safe place of adolescent mischief and benign rambunctiousness. It was a place of love gained and love lost all within the neon glow of a food court. The shopping mall ingratiated itself into American life and became far more intimate than the retail experiences before the rise of the mall.

Like many great projects of retail, John Wiebe began in earnest to please his wife. She had grown tired of driving to the traditional downtown central business district, fighting weather and traffic to do her shopping. Wiebe took to the skies in his small plane to survey Omaha for the perfect spot to build his epiphany. He found a 7 acre spot southwest of downtown Omaha. It was a strange rise in the land that locals often referred to as "dirt hill." From the unsightly hill Wiebe would help create an icon.

The Center rose up as a four level complex, the completely enclosed retail core being enveloped by a paring structure that wrapped around the building. The interior shopping area was climate controlled, warmed through the bitter Nebraska winter and cooled for the July heat. The concept of a shopping center, collectivized into a building with several different retailers sharing a community building was born.

John Wiebe's, Center Mall was a case of serendipity. A very similar style shopping center opened in Wisconsin just prior to the opening of the Omaha mall. Between the two, they were the first "Mall," in the United States and changed the way Americans purchase goods. The concept launched new businesses and torpedoes old and staid American businesses.

The Center remained a viable retail entity until it was damaged by fire in 1969. After 5 Million dollars in repairs, The Center re-opened with an Olde English in 1971 and was finally dubbed The Center Mall. It continued to function as a retail center into the 1990's when shifts in buying behavior and the migration of consumers farther west in Omaha. The Center transitioned from a retail center to an office and services center. Despite the change it has not been destroyed or changed. It's slightly older counterpart in Wisconsin has been torn down. So the first Mall in the United States still sits in Omaha. Hallways filled with the past emotions of buying clothes for a first date, or perhaps bonding with friends over a stack of crinkle fries at the restaurants. Maybe rolling a few strikes at the bowling alley for a family birthday. The mall means more to Americans than just clearance sales and black Fridays…they were a place to connect in different ways.

We have chronicled our collective connection to the shopping mall through a myriad of films. From. "Fast Times at Ridgemont High," to "Mallrats," we watched a subculture of

America live their lives in the mall. We were introduced to "Paul Blart: Mall Cop," and its sequel he sought to save his mall from robbery, while "Bad Santa," was looking to make his mall the mark for a robbery. In "Superbad," the boys find a way to break their codependence for the sake of growth and change. All of which seemed to take place at the mall, a uniquely American social institution.

The American shopping experience is changing, although the mall concept still exists, it is a dying breed, sustained only by the generations who want to look at a product before we buy. The rest of American consumers have embarked on a new type pf retail experience, one that provides a great river of goods and services directly to our homes. Consumers trade the social atmosphere and the event of going to the shopping mall for the convenience and price of receiving a product in the mail. The culture of the Mall still survives.

In Omaha, The Center Mall still stands, it continues to produce even if it has long since abandoned its retail beginnings. Maybe it was first, probably it was second, The Center Mall and the like became a catalyst for how commerce would function of the next 60 years. Today, as the age of the large commercial shopping center slowly bleeds to death and our commercial experiences become more and more private, the question will be, how do we connect as a people? Where do we go to see and be seen? Perhaps to where it all began in Omaha, Nebraska at The Center Mall.

Council Bluffs and a Modern Harvard

Reese Witherspoon made us laugh as a spoiled debutantes who worked her way into Harvard, in the film, "Legally Blonde." Matt Damon showed us that ability and merit can get you into any school in the film "Good Will Hunting." Harvard was not built on the egalitarianism and meritocracy that we think of today. It was not a school for women, Jews, or any other minorities. Harvard was consistently filled with the WASP-y legacies and old money children of New England affluence.

To go to Harvard meant going to the aged preparatory schools peppering the New England countryside. The exceptional scholar from the Midwestern rural community only dreamed of Harvard. Minorities of any type were a paucity at Harvard Yard. Harvard was simply a bastion of homogeneity and wealth prior to the early 1960's.

In 1953, a new wind blew in from the West. Harvard appointed a new president, the son of a grade school principle from Council Bluffs, IA, Nathan Pusey would now helm the venerable institution. The Pusey-era was a time that inclusion became the norm. Western students and African-American students suddenly became a part of the fabric of Harvard. Standardized test scores and school resume became the focus of admissions rather than the traditional recommendations of boarding schools. A great SAT might be the ticket into Harvard with Pusey as President, Harvard not only sought students from different backgrounds and areas of the countries but he also commissioned the admissions department to "look beyond brains." He pushed for students who were well-rounded in their development.

Along with his revision of who could actually attend Harvard, Pusey re-built Harvard financially and through construction. From 1953-1970, Harvard's budget quadrupled. Full time faculty tripled and he transformed the physical campus by adding over 30 buildings. With the growth of campus, Pusey expanded programs and needed new money to move Harvard forward in reputation and to make sure that it was the most important research University in America.

Pusey was ambitious in his role as president. He raised over $82 Million for the college and more than tripled the university endowment to over $1 Billion dollars. Harvard's fundraising efforts under Nathan Pusey were so successful that they became the model for how universities in the United States sought to raise money. Some of the activities and methods are still used today.

Pusey expanded scholarship and financial aid opportunities while expanding the number of Professors at the University. With a greater diversity of students being admitted and an increased number of professorships, Pusey also created a major increase in the number of scholarships offered to make Harvard accessible. Along with new admissions and greater inclusion, Pusey enacted something radical for the day. In 1963, with the intention of bringing the women's college, Radcliffe into the Harvard fold, allowed co-ed dorms and education. It was a sign of the times yet iconoclastic for many alumni. This was just one of the major social changes that faced Harvard in the Pusey era.

Harvard conferred an honorary degree on Hellen Keller in 1956. Henry Kissinger earned his doctorate and worked as a contemporary during the term of Nathan Pusey. Supreme Court Justice David Souter got his legal training in Cambridge. Actors John Lithgow and Tommy Lee

Jones trod the boards as Harvard. Tommy Lee Jones was one of the new breed who was able to come to Harvard due to Nathan Pusey's admissions overhaul. Jones lived across the hall from the son of a Tennessee Senator named Al Gore who would grow up to follow in his father's footsteps and climb just a little higher. Nathan Pusey resided over the creation of the Kennedy School of government which years later would educate one of the most important television personalities in America, Bill O'Reilly.

Pusey held the reigns at Harvard University just as the winds of change were blowing over the United States and the world. Communism was on the rise during the post-war years and it was creeping into areas throughout the world. In 1959, a young attorney who had been denied admission to Harvard in the late 1940's was able to depose President Fulgenico Batista of Cuba. Fidel Castro was invited to the Harvard Law School Forum to talk about his philosophies. Less than two years later it was Castro and another Harvard alum, John F. Kennedy who would go toe to toe in a battle of wills. The stakes were the fate of the world.

The 1960's were a time of social conflict and Harvard's stoic columns were not spared the changes. As the anti-war and anti-establishment movements became pre-eminent on campus, students became emboldened in their efforts at civil disobedience. In 1967, Secretary of Defense Robert McNamara visited campus to speak at the Institute of Politics. An anti-war student from Students for a Democratic Society was poised to debate McNamara but the Secretary was not interested in such interaction. To try and force the action, 800 students blocked Secretary McNamara's car, forcing him to escape through tunnels under the Harvard campus.

In 1967, a representative of war contractor Dow Pharmaceuticals was held hostage leading to several arrests, expulsions and hundreds of warnings. In 1968 students led a "Sit-In," when they were refused access to closed door meetings on ROTC at Harvard. The coup de grace to the problem came in 1969 after a group of students led by SDS entered and led an occupation of University Hall. The students were in the minority of the population but the continued actions of the students had become an embarrassment to Pusey and the rest of the Harvard administration.

The students were protesting the war and national policy vicariously through the university. The students demanded that ROTC be thrown off campus and as a minor demand, that an African-American studies program be implemented. The administration had no interest in negotiations.

Pusey called the authorities and in the early morning hours, the Boston Police Department led a raid on University Hall. The raid started at 5AM and was over by 5:25AM, the overzealous policemen had cleared University Hall but had left students and hallways a bloody mess.

In the aftermath, many of the students allied with SDS and voted to strike from classes. Neighboring schools joined in solidarity which put more pressure on the administration. The toll was great for Harvard. One of the academic deans suffered a stroke, others took a leave of absence. Harvard as a university had believed that it was somehow above the fray in regards to the social upheaval going on at Berkeley and Columbia. The 1969 takeover made Harvard aware that they too were subject to the iconoclastic era of the late 1960's. The last casualty of the takeover was Nathan Pusey. In 1970, two years before his retirement date, Pusey resigned over the affair.

In the end, Nathan Pusey transformed Harvard into a place that a talented student from anywhere in the country could study. He changed admissions from their focus on stodgy New England Prep schools, to a format where they seek well rounded students with exemplary standardized test scores. He incorporated African-Americans and created a Co-Ed experience at Harvard.

Pusey left Harvard in a powerful economic position and grew the campus through building and through students admitted. In the end, he made Harvard a dream possible to anyone in the country, not solely the wealthy legacies of Old New England. He also added scholarships and housing that benefitted all students. From Council Bluffs to Cambridge, Pusey brought egalitarianism to Harvard Yard.

Greetings from Omaha and the Birth of Viva Las Vegas.

It is hard to believe that in the 1940's, Las Vegas, Nevada was nothing but a small desert oasis with a few houses and a peculiar adherence to anachronistic laws more at home in the Old West than in modern America. Prostitution and Gambling had never been criminalized in Nevada as they had been in the rest of the United States. This reality made Nevada keenly interesting to the primary purveyors of gaming in the United States, the mafia.

During WWII, the Army created a Gunnery School near Las Vegas which would become Nellis Air Force Base after the war. It was here that Omaha native and Creighton University graduate, Jackie Gaughan, would first become accustomed to the possibilities that Las Vegas offered. Las Vegas did not get its start as a resort location until after WWII. Local gambling establishments had existed for decades but Benjamin Siegel changed the town forever when he built the Flamingo in 1946.

The Flamingo was created through a strange partnership between Bugsy Siegel, Meyer Lansky and Mormon Bankers. Meyer Lansky was a longtime crime partner and key player in Jewish Mafia Circles for decades. At the time the Flamingo was being planned and built, Lansky ran a Dog Track in Council Bluffs called the Dodge Park Kennel Club. Many of the funds from this track as well as others run by the mob were funneled to Las Vegas and into the dreams of Bugsy Siegel.

To be sure that the large amount of funds needed to fund the hotel and casino did not engage suspicion, mob financiers funneled the money through Mormon bankers plentiful in Nevada at the time. The Flamingo became a financial disaster when it was completed and resulted in the murder of Bugsy Siegel. The fortunes turned around after the Mafia took full control, they had just opened the Pandora's Box of the Las Vegas strip.

Jackie Gaughan returned to Las Vegas after learning the gambling industry from his family in Omaha. After changes in gambling laws in the early 1950's in Carter Lake, Iowa, Gaughan moved to Las Vegas to get involved with the fledgling resort town. Almost immediately after arriving in Nevada, Gaughan purchased a stake in the Flamingo hotel. Needless to say, at this time, the Mafia was still in firm control of the casino industry, especially that of Las Vegas.

Jackie soon purchased stakes in several, the l other casinos in Vegas including the Boulder Club. By the early 1960's he would acquire the Las Vegas Club and opened a new Casino-Hotel called the Western. Into the 1980's he ran the Gold Spike, the Golden Nugget, the Plaza, the Royal Inn and the Showboat. Jackie Gaughan became the king of the classic images of Vegas Casino glitterati. By the time he retired, he owned 25% of the downtown Las Vegas strip and various parcels of undeveloped land in the area.

In the late 1970's, Jackie's son Michael, also an Omaha native got in on the action and opened the Barbary Coast which has changed hands and is now the Cromwell. He later opened an off-strip hotel called the Gold Coast, he opened another in the 1980's called the Orleans, and at last in 2005 the South Point Hotel and Casino was completed in Las Vegas. Michael used Omaha architect Leo Daly to design the building. If you are flying to Las Vegas and you want to put a couple of coins in the slots at the airport, the money you lose will be going to Michael Gaughan.

The casinos that Gaughan created or owned were not the towering monoliths to gambling entertainment that we know today. Largely they were the pioneers of the industry and the casinos that made Ls Vegas Legendary. In the early 1970's, Jackie Gaughan became mentor to the man who helped create the modern image of Las Vegas. A young man named Steve Wynn acquired a majority share in the Golden Nugget and became the youngest casino owner in Las Vegas.

Wynn has since become one of the premier casino and resort owners in the world having expanded the Golden Nugget into a national chain as well as starting the Mirage, Treasure Island and the Bellagio, all premier resort locations on the Vegas strip.

Jackie Gaughan was a true pioneer of the casino industry so it makes sense that his casino roots has spread far and wide. Perhaps his best innovations that have lived on were his innovations that captured the hearts of Joe Sixpack. The average man was won over by many of Jackie's promotions including the Casino Funbook, Match play where the casino doubles the bettors winnings, and two for one specials.

Gaughan was able to fill his casinos on promotions even during slow times like holidays. He became the "King," of the value gambler. This innovation meant that casino gambling could be marketed to the masses as a means of entertainment rather than a pastime of serious big money gamblers which had been the focus of casinos prior to Jackie's efforts. This means the explosion of casino gambling that spread across the United States in the past 25 years into various areas was a product of Gaughan.

From Bookmaking in Carter Lake, Iowa and the horse tracks of Omaha. The Gaughan family has done as much as anyone to make gaming a part of the American experience. Gaughan's casinos have featured in a variety of American pop-culture scenes like Back to the Future films, James Bond movies, and a variety of television shows. This lends to the accessibility that Gaughan provided to his guests regardless of their status in life. Jackie Gaughan created a national industry out of the dust of an Old West watering hole. His successes have create an iconic worldwide image of the glamour and pleasure that we call, "Sin City."

How Radio Grew into the Biggest Mouse in the World

The early world of radio invention and innovation existed much like Silicon Valley nearly a century later. It was full of pirates and renegades, scrambling to create the next breakthrough. Each swindling the others around them in order to identify the next patentable breakthrough. The end result created modern radio technology and a myriad of other technologies which were stumbled upon during the buccaneering days of radio.

Lee de Forest received his PHd from Yale in 1899. He was immediately convinced that he was destined to be a rich and famous innovator. De Forest started his career working on a way to increase the speed of telegraphy. He wanted to increase the speeds that Morse code could be transmitted over long distances. His work is not unlike the modern effort of increasing download speeds.

Guglielmo Marconi and Nicola Tesla had gained considerable ground in radio invention in Europe about the same time. De Forest decided to focus on increasing the length that radio waves could be transmitted and received. His first innovations allowed signals to be transmitted about 4 miles. De Forest continued to experiment with radio technologies and created some minor innovations.

He intended to make money on these inventions and created his own company the Deforest Radio Telegraph Company. The company was dedicated to selling the radio equipment that de Forest invented and produced but it was rife with fraud and de Forest separated from the organization in 1906.

It was also in 1906 when de Forest created one of his most profound radio technologies, the Audion. The audion was important because it was the first invention that could detect a weak radio signal and amplify it to a stronger signal. This would become far more important later with efforts to perform long distance radio transmissions. The similarity between de Forest's work and the work of another radio scientist of the day, John Fleming. de Forest denied these similarities as preposterous, especially since the Fleming invention was used for something completely different than that of de Forest's Audion. Despite any similarities, the Patent courts gave Lee de Forest his patent in 1907.

In 1907, de Forest started the Radio-Telephone Company. de Forest's development of the Arc RadioTelephone allowed audio to be transmitted over long distances. This led to the first ship to shore transmissions. These were transmissions between ships on the water and a receiver on land. While the initial invention was unreliable and could not be used for consistent naval communications, it set the stage for communications to be made in all manner of transportation mediums.

With the increased experimentation of vacuum tubes, new discoveries flowed. In one experiment, de Forest recognized the reality of feedback while designing what he called the "Ultra-audion." Regenerative radio is the possibility of amplifying the radio waves and sending them over large distances. Edwin Armstrong also developed the concept and filed and received a patent for the discovery. After discovering this, de Forest also filed for a patent and the case ended in court. After the case rose all the way to the Supreme Court, de Forest was ultimately declared the patent holder.

With all the new innovation in radio it became feasible to finally create commercial broadcasts. de Forest commenced with building his radio station in New York City in 1915. This station was first in a number of things. It was the first to have a regular daily news broadcast. The station became a type of "wireless newspaper," and ran without restriction day and night. In 1916 the station became the first station to broadcast presidential election returns.

Amateur radio stations were ordered to be shut down during US involvement in WWI ending radio transmission until after the war. In 1919, the station re-opened and began with its programming but began playing limited phonograph recordings as well as its regular broadcasts.

In 1921, de Forest ran afoul with the authorities when he changed the location of his station without permission. In response to reprimand, de Forest took his transmitter and moved to California where he opened 6XC in San Francisco, California. De Forest claimed that this was the first radio station broadcasting to a public audience.

With the launch of the San Francisco station, de Forest worked to set up leasing deals with newspapers across the country who wanted to start their own radio stations. It also marked the end of de Forest's interest in radio experimentation. He set his sights on new technology and a new artistic medium that was exciting the nation. De Forest set out to solving the problem of a sound-on-film process.

De Forest had been working on this process for a while and originally filed a patent in 1919 for an optical sound on film process he called Phonofilm. By 1922, de Forest launched his product commercially and attempted to interest the Hollywood film industry in the new process. Unfortunately, de Forests success was limited in this area. Film producers largely ignored the innovation which resulted in de Forest trying to create a market by recording short films of vaudeville acts and cartoons which could be shown at independent theaters. This did not move the studios any closer to dealing with de Forest because the shorts did not make them believe the process would work on feature length films.

In 1927 after watching, "The Jazz Singer," the first feature length motion picture with sound, a young animator with big dreams was inspired to make an animated film with sound. The animator was Walt Disney and he and his brother Roy soon began production on "Steamboat Willie." There were no sound processes widely available so Walt searched far and wide for a process. Finally he worked with a respected film producer and distributor in New York City who had a process. Pat Powers was the distributor and his process was called Cinephone. But where did it come from?

Pat Powers was an investor with de Forest's Phonofilm at the time. In the mid to late 1920's, de Forest sought to claim inventions as his own from collaborators which created a falling out and eventual lawsuits. After severing ties with the former partners, de Forest found himself in financial hardship which made him a target for the cut-throat Pat Powers. Powers moved in immediately and tried to take over Phonofilm from de Forest. De Forest was able to fight off the takeover but in the meantime, Power hired away, William Garity, a Phonofilm technician from de Forest. Garity cloned the Phonofilm process and called it Cinephone.

Steamboat Willie was largely a musical production that used limited voices. The soundtrack was provided by an Omaha, Nebraska based band, the Green Brothers Novelty Band. The band would continue to work on Walt Disney's first three cartoons all employing the Green Brothers distinctive Ragtime sound.

The first cartoon to bring about Mickey Mouse used a stolen sound process created by Lee de Forest and Steamboat Willie was an instant success. Unfortunately for de Forest, he was in too weak a financial position to launch a legal challenge to Cinephone and Disney Studios continued to use the process until 1940.

This would not be the only time that Disney looked for Omaha talent in its search for the best. After Steamboat Willie, Disney was a bona fide producer of film shorts. The company began production on shorts that told different stories. Disney called these musical shorts, Silly Symphonies. They were shown before and after film features at movie theaters.

In 1933, after a run of successful shorts, Disney began in earnest to produce, "The Three Little Pigs." The plot was based on the classic fable of the same name replete with three pigs, with three building styles and one nefarious wolf. The difference in this version was that it was a musical. To provide the Lyrics and music, Disney tapped Omaha born Ann Ronell to organize the music. What she created was exceptional!

"The Three Little Pigs," Silly Symphony was released in 1933 and included the song, "Who's Afraid of the Big Bad Wolf." Theater goers reveled over the short and drove the popularity of Disney productions ever higher. The short became the most financially successful animated short ever made. It was so successful that it earned Disney the 1934 Academy Award for Best Animated Short Film, their first Oscar. The financial success attracted other producers to follow a similar model and inspired such new animation productions as Warner Brothers Looney Tunes and Merrie Melodies. That means without Disney and Ann Ronell's masterpiece, we would not have Bugs Bunny and crew. Courtesy of a lady from Omaha. Silly Symphonies also used the stolen de Forest process.

Lee de Forest was married four times in his life and as if this story needed another Omaha connection, he married his last wife, Marie Mosquini in 1930. Marie was the ingénue for Hal Roach Studios in Hollywood. Marie acted alongside another Omaha, NE star Harold Lloyd. The spectacled actor who thrilled audiences by hanging from the hands of a clocktower.

In the end, Lee de Forest created innovations that gave rise to almost all radio controlled devices including Walkie Talkies, Toy cars, and all manner of communication.

When you go to your car in the morning and click on the morning news, just remember for a few seconds that Lee de Forest and legions of piratical capitalists made it happen. When you set your child in front of the electronic babysitter to watch a Disney film for the millionth time, it was de Forest and a band from Omaha that made that success happen. The invisible hand of Omaha moved the worked with the creation of Disney. This is not just moving American culture, but creating a worldwide icon.

5
Omaha: Mother of Hollywood!

She could not have known as she sang, "La Carioca," that she was creating a full circuit to Omaha, Nebraska. Mexican-American Actress Movita Castaneda lent her exotic beauty and dulcet singing voice for the first song Fred Astaire and Ginger Rogers would dance to on film.

It was all for the 1933 RKO Pictures film, "Flying Down To Rio." Fred Astaire, the son of an Austrian beer salesman who once worked for Storz Brewery in Omaha, Nebraska, tapped his way to stardom and became part of the Golden Age of Hollywood. In 1960, Movita Castaneda would become Mrs. Marlon Brando and complete the circle for the Omaha connection, as Omaha is the hometown of the famous actor.

RKO Pictures built and owned the Orpheum Theater in Downtown Omaha which still stands today. The RKO company is being run by CEO Ted Hartley, an Omaha native. This is just a small part of Omaha's prodigious connections to the Hollywood TV and Film Industry. The Omaha tendrils grew into the industry from the beginning and have never slowed nor receded.

The beginnings of Hollywood and the American motion picture industry commenced when Gurdon Wattles built his summer home in the placid Hollywood Hills as he prepared for his retirement. As movie makers made California their permanent headquarters in the late teens and into the 1920's. Wattles became the money man for the early masterpieces of the film genre including, "Birth of a Nation," by DW Griffith. Harold Lloyd and Harry Langdon became silent film giants from humble beginnings in the metro-area. They were the contemporaries of several Omaha actors and actresses like Clarence Barr and Eva Thatcher, who worked in film with lesser-fame during the era

Inventor Lee DeForest gave sound to many early films. His invention was used to create the Disney empire. Disney drew from the cultural energy of Omaha for decades. In 1955, Omaha-born voice actor George Givot played Tony in Lady and the Tramp, connecting Omaha to one of the most beloved animated scenes in movie history. Who can forget Lady and the Tramp sharing an ersatz "kiss," with the assistance of an incredibly long Spaghetti noodle?

People from Omaha have revolutionized the movie industry, creating such icons as King Kong and Mighty Joe Young, while also helping to popularize the concept of nature and culture documentaries. Others created the concept of "race" films which influenced the film industry from decades after they burst on the scene and decades longer than original Race films were necessary. In time, these Hollywood innovations would influence other types of entertainment and become a part of almost all American homes.

Dodie Brando was a stage actress and the mother of Marlon Brando. She was also a theater administrator who helped organize the Omaha Community Playhouse into a prolific font of Hollywood acting talent. One of Omaha's favorite sons, Henry Fonda at the Omaha Community Playhouse. Not long after he found his fame on the New York Stage and not long after he found himself on the big screen. Fonda starred alongside Movita Brando in the 1948 film Fort Apache, again creating the complete Omaha circuit. Fonda was the progenitor of an acting legacy in his children who were both powerful and controversial in their talents. There is little doubt that they have influenced modern American culture.

The Omaha Community Playhouse also helped produce such talents as Dorothy McGuire who would later star in the Disney film, "Old Yeller," as the mother, as the Virgin Mary in the Greatest Story Ever Told and as Mother Robinson in another Disney Classic, "Swiss Family Robinson." McGuire also starred in the controversial, "Gentleman's Agreement," opposite Gregory Peck. The film has another area connection as it was produced by Wahoo, Nebraska born, Darryl Zanuck.

Marlon Brando became a natural actor at a very young age. Dodie was an alcoholic and Marlon learned to mimic his surrounding and people he encountered as a way to distract his mother from drinking. He of course grew to be one of the greatest film actors in history creating iconic characters and performances that cannot be replicated. He won the Oscar twice, the first for, "On the Waterfront, in 1954 and then again in 1972 for his role as Don Vito Corleone in, "The Godfather." The Godfather film is considered one of the greatest films ever made and returned Marlon Brando to elite status in the motion picture industry.

Brando would not be our last connection to Hollywood. Starting in the 1990's, an Omaha-born director began to make his mark with films he chose to make in his hometown. Alexander Payne made his first feature-length film, "Citizen Ruth," a lesson on the moral and legal ambiguity that abortion deals with in American culture. Payne would follow this film with several critically acclaimed films and two Oscars. Film would not be the only foray of Omaha talent. The silver screen was also a zenith to be conquered and America was captured by the stars of Omaha, Nebraska.

Johnny Carson became an American institution. Johnny was a king-maker who launched a thousand careers. American's watched as Johnny entertained throughout the years and lived his private life in a very public forum. Paula Zahn reported the tragic events of September 11th, 2001 to America and the world from her anchor's chair at CNN but she started life in Omaha. The Simpson's have had several connections to Omaha including Milhouse's grandmother, and a visit from Hall of Fame Third Baseman Wade Boggs. Jorge Garcia may play characters living on Pacific islands like he does currently in the CBS program Hawaii Five-O and on the ABC phenomenon "Lost."

Omaha even has a connection to Country-Pop superstar Taylor Swift. Besides her tunes invading the radio, Taylor is the godmother to Leo Thames King-Newman. Second son of Omaha-born model and actress Jaime King. Omaha is well represented in the entertainment community and is truly the progenitor for the entire establishment of the movie industry.

Omaha Stars IN!: Creating Hollywood!

In Hollywood today, Nebraska is flyover country. So often people from Nebraska are thought of as unwashed yokels that do not have the class or sophistication to understand the movie industry. Big Movie producers and directors may see Omaha as a speck of light when they make their cross country flight to New York City. They would never make films about Nebraska, because who the hell would want to go to Nebraska, or even Omaha?

Except, the existence of modern Hollywood is based on people and activities that all happened in the heartland. The conception of a film metropolis may not have been visible from the cornfields, nor did the smell of the stockyards make people dream of the glamour of La La Land, but it was here that dream factory truly began.

In 1893, Thomas Edison created the kinetoscope, dazzling audiences wherever it was displayed. Soon, moving picture shows were being watched all over the country. Films would be shown in an old barn or a large room. Since, Thomas Edison controlled the patent and the output of his device, films of the day were restricted to dancing girls and animal acts. The creative process of film making would not be recognized in the beginning.

In 1898, Gurdon Wattles was the leader of the Trans-Mississippi Festival in Omaha. It was a spectacle to remove the shadow from the states West of the Mississippi. Wattles brought the Edison machine to Nebraska and captured some of the earliest images of a US President on film when President William McKinley was making his entrance. It is amazing to think that McKinley was a Civil War veteran and the first president to be in a motion picture.

Gurdon Wattles became enamored with the concept of motion pictures and continued to promote the idea of making films of Nebraska for display at events around the country. His idea was to create a video advertisement of what Nebraska could offer tourists and people seeking a new place to live. In short, he created the first motion picture advertisements of anything.

Wattles had distinguished himself at the Trans-Mississippi Exposition and made the event the most financially successful world's Fair of the era. When St. Louis hosted their World's Fair in 1904, the Governor of Nebraska looked to Wattles to again head the production of the Nebraska entry. Over the next year, Wattles commissioned several films of Nebraska life to be made. He would be showing the short clips to visitors to the Nebraska Pavilion at the fair.

Because over 10,000 feet of film were shot and this included several different scenes, viewers could return to the pavilion and see something new each time they visited. The most popular films were those of President McKinley and those of rodeo riders working on a cattle ranch. With an average of 2000 visitors per day visiting Wattle's theater devoted to Nebraska was a success.

The films were such a success that they were passed on to the next World's Fair held in Portland , Oregon the following year. It is unclear what the fate of these films was after the Portland fair but they have been lost to time and memory. If they were not converted or preserved in some unknown collection, they would be destroyed by natural consequences of time. The Nebraska Life Movie exhibit was the first type of display of its kind to ever be presented but this would not be the last connection of Gurdon Wattles to the film industry. First he would become the mass transit king of Omaha!

Wattles returned to Omaha and continued the shrewd brand of business that had made him a standout among men at in turn of the century Nebraska. Prior to Wattle's activities at the fairs, he had become the most important mover and shaker in Omaha. In 1890, he cornered the market on the mass transit in Omaha by consolidating his properties with others that he controlled or acquired. His new company became the Omaha Traction Company and it quickly became the pre-eminent mass transit company in Omaha and Council Bluffs. Labor began to recognize its power at the turn of the century and the consolidation actually handed Labor Unions a high card in the first decade of the 1900's.

As Unions worked to organize the Omaha Traction company workers, Gurdon Wattles recognized the problem new Unions could cause a variety of industries in Omaha. He had already seen unions organize over 70 Locals in the area and now feared they would consume his company too. Wattles quickly organized the Omaha Business Men's Association with a sole purpose of protecting the open Shop Status that classically existed in Omaha.

In a short time, Gurdon Wattles claimed he had over 800 retailers and wholesalers in Omaha on board with the Business Men's Association on a mission to keep Omaha as the "…best open shop city of its size in the United States." The new association looked like it was bailing against the tide as new trade unions were being formed each week during the era. Some news outlets even claimed that Omaha was one of the, "Most thoroughly organized union cities in the United States." The Business Men's Association realized that taking on the unions in the biggest industries might have been foolish. For these reasons, railroad and meatpacking unions were largely ignored by the OBMA.

The BMA announced their intentions in early business friendly newspapers like Edward Rosewater's Omaha Bee. They declared that they wanted to end the strikes but not the right of workers to unionize. They quickly outlined their platform. First: Freedom to employ Union and Non-Union Labor, Second: No Limitation to output and Third: No sympathy strikes.

The BMA worked to help companies to weather union organizing, strikes and other union activities. The group also helped to organize legal and legislative aid meant to stymie the zealous efforts of organized labor of the period. The association was very effective in their efforts and limited large scale gains by labor in the first tears of the 1900's. Labor Unions weren't ready to go softly into the night. The efforts of the Unions in Omaha and the stress Gurdon Wattles endured made him think about consider time away.

The stress of this time period wore on Wattles and after a visit to California with his wife, Wattles started work on a vacation home and eventually a retirement retreat for himself in a tiny new suburb of Las Angeles, California. His summer home would was a Mediterranean/Mission Revival mansion with avocado and citrus trees and a collection of formal gardens, including the first Japanese Garden in the United States. He explained his interest in the area thusly:

> *"The next spring we went back; this time we found the usual sunshine and soft air, and were so charmed that I determined to buy and improve a place, so when the time came for me to quit work I would have a home for rest and relaxation. I had always remembered the high hill and creek flowing down through a depression, making a series of waterfalls, which was behind my childhood home at Padlock, New York. Many years spent on the prairies of the Middle West had brought a desire to live again near the mountains. With the help of a friend, I selected and purchased ninety acres in Hollywood, a suburb of Los Angeles."*

Construction began in 1905, Wattles would continue to work on the grounds for several more years but it was ready to live in by 1907; just as it was sorely needed for the avaricious entrepreneur from Omaha would need a place to escape his self-imposed exile.

By 1909, the Omaha Traction Company had its own organized union but for Gurdon Wattles they were about to step over the line. Gurdon Wattles was traditionally a friend of the working man but he despised organized labor tactics, and when the union made a play for a closed shop at Wattle's Omaha Traction Company, he saw his chance to rid himself of the meddlesome organization.

When Wattles refused to consider this demand, the Union voted to strike which played directly into Wattle's plans. He immediately shipped in strikebreakers from New York City to act as muscle and to work as scabs, replacement workers employed in place of striking workers. Wattle's tactics did not go unnoticed by his colleagues and while he had some support, there were many who privately urged him to negotiate with the Unions. His hard line hurt his status with the average man in Omaha and society overall. Once the most respected man in Omaha, Gurdon Wattles began to see his personal stock begin to flag.

The union wanted a "closed shop," a closed shop exists when management is required to hire employees that are union members. Essentially, the Union controls all personnel decisions in a closed shop. This was not something Gurdon Wattles would negotiate. A union that was seeking that level of power in his company would have to go. The Union would make one last effort to overcome Wattle's strikebreaking efforts.

In September 1909, the striking streetcar workers made it known that they were not intimidated by Wattle's Hired goons. Up to 1500 workers stormed the railcars and the offices of the Omaha Traction Company, rioting and destroying property. Fighting broke out between strikers and strikebreakers throughout downtown Omaha. Customers largely backed the streetcar workers and refused to ride or give the company any fares during the strike. The riots were finally contained after 4 days of wanton destruction, but the hard truth about economics settled on the members of the union.

The strikers, recognizing that competing with cheap labor Wattles had on hand to take their jobs represented an obstacle that they could not overcome. Within a couple of weeks, the union was shattered and the majority of the strikers returned to their old jobs. Wattles would only allow them to return if they were no longer members of the Union. Gurdon Wattles did what he set out to do, to rid his Omaha Traction Company of what he thought of as a scourge. Wattles had achieved such a state of self-satisfaction that he wrote a book talking about the strike, his success, and his general philosophy of how labor should be controlled moving forward. Despite what he considered a personal and business success, the Gurdon Wattles name was heavily damaged and his personal reputation tarnished during the episode. He needed an escape...

Wattles felt as though he had found an enemy in his own hometown. He felt he had been beset with socialists and elements of anarchy. With his fortune still amassed in his Omaha interests, he began taking extended vacations to the new summer home just north of downtown Las Angeles. His new home was in the newly incorporated town of Hollywood, CA, home to fruit and vegetable orchards and absolutely no movie stars. Gurdon Wattles made money wherever he went and tiny, bucolic, piece of Southern California would be no different. Wattles was a banker, and finance would be the key to a whole new kingdom.

By 1920, Wattles had moved full-time to Hollywood. He had been a frequent and long-time resident since 1909. Events in New Jersey had transplanted a new industry to California. Thomas Edison vociferously controlled the patents on most motion picture technology which meant those interested in filmmaking could not generally complete feature length films, nor could they seek outside financing. It all changed when potential directors pulled up stakes from New Jersey and headed to Hollywood. In California, Edison could no longer enforce is patents. Gurdon Wattles was free to invest in the new media.

By 1912, most filmmakers in the United States had relocated to the small northern suburb of LA. In 1915, when DW Griffith made the first feature film in Hollywood, "Birth of a Nation," it was Omaha-born, Joseph Henabery who starred as Abraham Lincoln. Henabery went on to act and direct in several later Griffith pictures. It was said to be a masterpiece of theatre makeup of the time. Henabery would later direct for several of the early Hollywood studios with stars such as Rudolph Valentino, Douglas Fairbanks and Fatty Arbuckle

Back in Omaha, Wattles convinced a friend Phil Goldstone to make his home on the coast. The two financed a variety of the earliest Hollywood films and speculated in property all over Los Angeles. Years later, Goldstone's nephew, "Duke," relocated and started as a prop boy for the early movie studios, eventually working his way up to director. He was prolific television director in the 1950's working on the original "Dick Tracy," television program in 1951 and Betty White's first sit-com. He was also the first director of "The Lawrence Welk Show."

Wattles continued his professional activities late in life. Much of his fortune was devastated during the economic crash of 1929. Wattles died at his Hollywood property in 1932. His family continued to live at the property until his wife died in 1977.

The property would later become the property of the City of Los Angeles to be used as a park and event center. It will always be remembered as one of the first full-time homes in Hollywood. A place where the money flowed and created the industry that Hollywood is so famous for. To think…the show started in Omaha…America's Hometown…FADE TO BLACK.

It was Beauty that Killed the Beast!

A child of the 1980's recognizes its tinny symphonic trance in seconds. The soundtrack of their young lives represents a daily friend that many were loath to give up even into adulthood. Many who have moved on to more adult practices still sneak back to childhood to connect with the old Italian time burglar who haunts their dreams. What am I talking about you ask? The legendary Super Mario Brothers. It was the game that introduced us to the challenges of romance and the dangers of strange turtles and the power that some mushrooms had when consumed by electronic heroes. This was the magical world that the Nintendo Entertainment System created for millions of American children.

You may be thinking, "That is great Scott, but there is NO way that Nintendo has anything to do with the Omaha metro area." To that I say, you underestimate the nerdery that consumes my brain. Video Game buffs are quick to note that Nintendo is a Japanese video game manufacturer and Omaha is not in Japan. You are right, but Omaha didn't create video games, and they didn't build any of them either. No, Omaha was the muse which launched the product into the home of every Soccer Mom in America.

We have to go back to the early 1980's. Video games were reaching almost epidemic status in the United States. A person could go to almost any location and find one or two units set up in a corner with a couple of kids plugging quarters into them. Soon parents started to become concerned that these amusements were not good for their children and challenged the fledgling gaming industry by refusing to buy any of the dozens of different gaming systems that began to flood the market. This created a crash that put many companies out of the market forever. One inventive company had timed the market just right and had created a game that America loved. Leaving this company with overflowing coffers.

With the rest of the gaming world in shambles, Nintendo rode the back of an ape and a plumber to the top of the industry. In 1981 Shimeru Miramoto designed the game Donkey Kong which was the hit that Ninetendo needed to conquer the world. The next step was eliminating the expense of the upright console and taking the console directly into the home. With their Donkey Kong Money, Nintendo went directly to research and development mode to create the Nintendo Entertainment System. The console sold millions and Mario multiplied as quickly as the Nintendo sold. But what does this have to do with Omaha?

Nintendo was under some pressure. They tried to develop a Popeye game but their license ran out. Miramoto needed something that would connect with Americans. He came up with Donkey Kong which was not very far from the concept that he lifted the idea from, "King Kong." "King Kong," is a worldwide icon and Miramoto knew it! It all started with a couple of buddies and a camera. First they had to live through WWI!

American involvement in the "Great War," started in 1917 and Ernest Schoedsack signed up to do his part. His part was to be the Videographer for the US Army. Maybe it was just the war fever or maybe it was his upbringing that made him volunteer, but the tall lanky boy from Council Bluffs, IA became the one to record the earliest videos known of Americans at war. His work during the war taught him his craft well and after the war he met Merian Cooper who would become his longtime partner in films. Together the two would devise an entirely new concept of nature and sociology documentaries. These first ventures made them noteworthy, but their joint collaboration about a giant ape released in 1933 made them world famous. King Kong has been re-made at least three times and the story is known around the world. It was this film Shigeru Miramoto used to design his most famous game.

If you are thinking that a Council Bluffs guy isn't exactly from Omaha, well that is obviously correct. But this story doesn't simply end with Edwin Schoedsack, there is a direct Omaha connection and one that takes us to another piece of American culture. The 1970's!!!

In the 70's a film genre swept the film industry and millions still remember these types of films as a quintessential memory of the 1970's. With all Black casts and often campy storylines, Blaxploittion was a technique that got its start decades before and continued to find success decades after the last ticket was sold for Shaft. The whole concept of an African-American cast and themes from this community was rooted, not in the free market exactly but in necessity.

In the early years of cinema, African-Americans largely were not allowed to visit movie theaters and watch films with a mixed audience. Most of the films of the day were created for the white viewer as well. That changed with the creation of what was called the "Race Film." These were films created by African-Americans for African-Americans. The theaters were often barns or other cheaply procured community buildings and the single copy productions would often be forced to travel from town to town to be shown. What does this have to do with King Kong or Omaha?

The inventor of race films and the first owner of an all-black studio was an Omaha man named Noble Johnson. Noble started the Lincoln Motion Picture Company in 1916 and produced films until 1921. As Noble gained stature in the film industry of the early years, he started getting noticed for mainstream movie roles. In 1933, Shoedsack and Cooper noticed Noble Johnson for a part in King Kong. Noble played the Native chief on Skull Island in the film. He went on to play in dozens of films but we cannot forget that his concept helped create the career of Bill Cosby in the 1980's and of Will Smith as the "Fresh Prince of Bel-Air," in the 1990's

Ernest Schoedsack continued to make Kong films. He also made the film "Mighty Joe Young," again, about an ape. It was a long way from his beginnings in Hollywood as a cameraman for Mack Sennett where he may have shot film of Harry Langdon a star from Council Bluffs, Iowa, the Keystone Cops or maybe even Sennett's Provocative Bathing Beauties. Every road and every strip of film led Schoedsack back home to America's Hometown…Omaha!

Michael Jackson's REAL Father?

So many stories in Omaha begin with the pursuit of beer! In the late 1800's Omaha was blessed with several large beer concerns. It was the Storz brewery that starts off our story. Gottlieb Storz had a large brewery and several "sampling rooms" around town. Storz had his bars but Omaha was lousy with bars and there were several beer companies who wanted the market share. So, Storz took on a new salesman for Omaha, an Austrian named Frederic "Fritz" Austerlitz.

Fritz moved his wife to South 10th St. in Omaha and promptly started a family.

Fritz was good at his game which allowed him to travel throughout the Midwest. Meanwhile his wife dreamed of her children being in show business and started them off with dance lessons. She saw them becoming a sibling dance act, a common act in the early days of vaudeville. Fritz named his boy Fred, after himself but as his children grew in entertainment community they changed their very Germanic sounding last name to Astaire. Fred Astaire and his older sister Adele learned several musical instruments while they perfected their dance steps.

Throughout the years of entertaining, Fred and Adele became more and more polished with their abilities and their dance routines. Fred learned to tap dance and this form was implemented into the routine. This was an accompaniment to the waltz, tango and other traditional ballroom dances they had already added to the act. Fred was constantly looking for new steps and ideas to add to the show. He believed the audience always wanted novelty, something new in their entertainment. The Astaire siblings didn't do anything half-way, when they added a new routine, they sought perfection in themselves and this quality endeared them to their audiences.

In 1933, Fred and his sister found their way to California and into an RKO Screen test. Fred's results were the stuff of legend. The report stated that Astaire, "Can't act, slightly bald, also dances." Although Astaire was signed by RKO pictures, it took the President of the studio to step in with a memo in Astaire's defense. David O. Selznick wrote, "I am uncertain about the man, but I feel, in spite of his enormous ears and bad chin line, that his charm is so tremendous that it comes through even on this wretched test."

Astaire was soon coupled with Ginger Rogers and the two made several musicals throughout the 1930's and in the process danced into the hearts of the American people. The two became renowned for their dancing although Astaire usually received more attention for his dancing prowess. Rogers was quoted as saying, "I did everything Fred Astaire could except I did it backwards and in high heels."

Fred Astaire danced through almost 50 years of movie and television stardom. An area that he was never given much credit for was his signing ability, however he was often called upon to sing in his films as well. Astaire insisted he could not sing, however many of the songwriters and other musicians who were his contemporaries tended to laud his performance. Additionally, some of his music even made it to the top of the music charts of the day.

If you listened to the comments from Astaire, he was not the greatest singer OR dancer of the century. That honor belonged to his "descendant." Shortly after playing in his final film, a retired Fred Astaire discovered the talents of a young man who was beginning to become a superstar. The young man was Michael Jackson who had developed a dance style by borrowing moves and paying homage to the great dancers of the past which included Fred Astaire.

Fred Astaire contacted Michael Jackson after seeing him in the televised "Motown 25" special and told the young King of Pop:

> *"You're a hell of a mover. Man, you really put them on their asses last night," Fred Astaire told Michael Jackson. "You're an angry dancer. I'm the same way. I used to do the same thing with my cane."*
>
> *Jackson replied, "It was the greatest compliment I had ever received in my life and the only one I had ever wanted to believe."*

In later interviews Astaire would continue his opinion of Jackson's abilities by proclaiming, *" Oh, God! That boy moves in a very exceptional way. That's the greatest dancer of the century".* Seeing the end of his life coming and knowing that his own children would not follow him into show business or in dancing. Fred expressed one last sentiment of love for Michael Jackson's talent and ability. He called him a son….well….something like that.

"I didn't want to leave this world without knowing who my descendant was. Thank you Michael!"

For his part, Michael was overwhelmed by Astaire's support for him. So much so that when Astaire died in 1987, Michael dedicated his 1988 autobiography, "Moonwalk," to the memory of Fred Astaire.

From Omaha in the 1890's, Astaire grew from a son of a beer salesman to a huge box office draw. He influenced generations of dancers singers and actors. Astaire's biggest influence may have been on the King of Pop, Michael Jackson, who Astaire called his "descendant."

Astaire continues to find his way into popular culture. Shortly after his death, recorded footage from an old movie was used to create a vacuum cleaner commercial, of course Ginger Rogers had to become the vacuum so Astaire could exuberantly dance with a vacuum but so be it. We also saw Astaire dance again, which amazed John Coffey, the Angelic but condemned main character in the Stephen King film, "The Green Mile." Fred Astaire keeps making his mark on American culture even in death. From the first tap steps on South 10th Street in Omaha, Fred helped make Omaha, America's Hometown.

Heeeere's Johnny!

> *"And so it has come to this: I, uh... am one of the lucky people in the world; I found something I always wanted to do and I have enjoyed every single minute of it. I want to thank the people who've shared this stage with me for thirty years. Mr. Ed McMahon, Mr. Doc Severinsen, and you people watching. I can only tell you that it has been an honor and a privilege to come into your homes all these years and entertain you. And I hope when I find something that I want to do and I think you would like and come back, that you'll be as gracious in inviting me into your home as you have been. I bid you a very heartfelt good night."* Johnny Carson on his final Tonight Show Broadcast

That is how one of the greatest television stars in American history ended his reign as the "king of Late Night." It was the end of a lifetime of entertaining people and the majority of it spent in front of a live studio audience.

Johnny Carson grew up in Nebraska and at a very young age drifted towards entertainment. He became the "Great Carsoni," to entertain his family and his mother's Bridge Club. His first paid gigs were at the local civic clubs and county fairs. He turned 18 in 1943 as the world was at war, so instead of starting out in the entertainment business, he joined the Navy to serve his country. In 1945, Carson was steaming toward Japan on a troop ship when the bombs fell on Hiroshima and Nagasaki which ended the war.

After the war, he went back to Nebraska and became a Nebraska Cornhusker where he majored in Journalism. He wasn't a Cornhusker as long as most students, he flew through his program. He graduated by submitting a final thesis entitled, "How to Write Comedian Jokes." His career in entertainment started in 1950 when he took his first job as a radio host at WOW. He also served as a disc jockey on WOW radio, where he would often butcher the commercials of such local advertisers such as the Friendly Savings Bank for comedic effect. Carson soon made his way to TV at the same station when he was given an early afternoon radio program called, "Squirrel's Nest."

"Squirrel's Nest," was a comic variety show. Johnny told jokes and monologue with the audience, he also came up with funny skits and gags.

> *"I can remember back in Omaha when I was doing a local show, we used to play bridge on television. I thought it was a clever idea. We had these jumbo cards. I'd have two guests come up, and we'd sit there and I'd call a lady at home, Mrs. So-and-So, and I'd hold the hand up to the camera, and she'd play it."*

The program became a kind of boot camp for what would become his life's work. One such ongoing gag where Carson would interview the pigeons roosted on top of the Omaha city hall. The bit resulted in general ribbing of local politicians and dignitaries. This was something completely out of character for Johnny when he graduated to the Tonight Show, where he never talked politics.

> *"I did a thing once when they were trying to get rid of the pigeons on the county courthouse, and I took the pigeons' side and I went on top of the building and sat there talking to the pigeons."*

In 1950, it made enough people laugh that Johnny was encouraged to create an audition video of his best stuff. He took it on vacation with him and shopped it out to various television stations in LA and San Francisco. His fishing expedition was fruitless until a family friend called in a favor from a relative working at KNXT-TV in LA. The recommendation turned into a low-budget Sunday afternoon comedy show called Carson's Cellar. (Clips are still available on YouTube.)

From here, Johnny spent the next 10 years with ups and downs in the TV industry. In the early 1960's, Carson occasionally filled in for Jack Paar who was the original star of the Tonight Show. Paar had grown weary of the daily grind of the show and did not want to continue. He publicly promoted Johnny on the show and finally NBC offered him a contract and the rest is history.

Johnny went on to star on The Tonight Show for the next 30 years. He made millions of people laugh and created the careers of several others including Jay Leno, Roseanne Barr, Steven Wright, Drew Carey, Joan Rivers, Jerry Seinfeld, David Letterman, Ellen DeGeneres, Eddie Murphy, Bill Maher, Jim Carrey, George Carlin, and a variety of others. Needless to say, the family tree of talent connected to Johnny Carson is mammoth and continues to grow.

Johnny Carson became a mighty oak in television which grew from an acorn buried at the "Squirrels Nest," in Omaha, NE. Today there are many late night programs from the classic networks to cable networks. The medium of late night talk shows was proven by Johnny Carson and after David Letterman, one of his protégé's, launched a competing late night talk show and showed that the market was hot for greater competition the television world has spawned dozens of options.

Johnny Carson climbed the ladder to superstardom in New York and Los Angeles. He noted that he owed his career to a bunch of pigeons that he talked to on his first rung of the ladder in Omaha, NE.

Omaha...Full of Characters

There is no place like home. Countless children over generations have learned this from the movie made from L. Frank Baum's classic book series featuring the Wizard of Oz. Of course, Baum's stories were set in Kansas with Dorothy and Toto being the primary heroines. Their goal was to meet the Wizard of Oz. A mysterious wizard who appeared out of nowhere.

In the novel, the Wizard uses a variety of tricks to hide his identity. He uses illusions and magic tricks to conceal his true identity, he is finally found out to be a circus magician from Omaha, NE named Oscar Zoroaster Phadrig Isaac Norman Henkle Emmannuel Ambroise Diggs. The Oz exploits spanned several books and became massively popular throughout the United States because of their rendition in plays amd most famously in the 1939 film starring Judy Garland. Through them all, the Great and Powerful Oz was nothing but a magician and a con-man from Omaha, NE.

Just because the Wizard didn't have any powers outside of illusion doesn't mean we don't have others from Omaha with superhuman powers. Kansas may have Superman, New York may have Spiderman, but Omaha has one of the X-Men. Scott Summers the First of the X-Men, according to the comic book, was born in Alaska but was orphaned after his family was attacked by aliens while flying their small plane. Scott suffered a head injury and spent most of his childhood at the State Home for the Foundlings in Omaha, Nebraska. The home was more of a secret lab where Dr. Sinister created mutant children, something between Boys Town and Offutt Air Force Base. Maybe they will explain that a little more in the next movie.

Omaha also has its odd, quirky everymen who have been part of the lives of millions of television and movie viewers. Warren Schmidt shows us the tragic and comical side of retirement from a grand old Omaha profession. He reluctantly retires from an Insurance company and goes on a voyage of self-discovery. His story told through inappropriate letters to young African boy he has "adopted," through a television commercial. In the end, it is his connection he had made with the little boy who helps him recognize that he has helped to impact the life of others.

Warren Schmidt is a character created by Oscar-award winning director and Omaha-native Alexander Payne. Omaha tends to be one of his favorite subjects in his films and another of his characters comes from "Election." Reese Witherspoon stars as the libidinous, overachiever, Tracy Flick. Circumstances and politics put her at war with Mr. McCallister and the opponent he picks to try and steal her thunder. Tracy is smart, devious and manipulative and is a worthy match. While Tracy Flick was the overachiever with all the gifts, Omaha TV characters are not nearly the foils.

In the 1990's, it was Aunt Becky, the girlfriend of John Stamos' Uncle Jesse on the hit television program "Full House." She entered the program as a news anchor having moved from a fictional morning TV show, A.M. Omaha. She quickly became the feminine voice of reason for the growing girls who were otherwise raised ably by a team of men. She has returned with the age of the internet as new episodes of the long running 1990's program have been created called "Fuller House." Perhaps not the hit it once was, Aunt Becky is still an Omaha girl.

The Simpsons have been a part of American life for 27 years. Over such a long time, we learn a lot about the characters who remain perpetually the same age. In Season 16, Bart Simpson finds a cache of discarded "Playdude Magazines," and chooses to adopt a devil-may-care Hugh Hefner style lifestyle based on the things he finds. He enlists his best friend Milhouse Van Houten who after hearing that stewardesses may offer a "layover," expresses his wish that the layover be in Omaha so he can see his grandmother. Omaha connections abound in The Simpson's, Omaha-born stage and film actor, Andrew Rannels portrayed himself in a 2016 episode.

The latest character has proven that nerds are lovable throughout the world. Kaley Cuoco Penny is a character from one of the most popular shows on TV today, the Big Bang Theory. Kelly Cuoco created a character who, while not as formally educated as the rest of the cast displays superior social and emotional intelligence which becomes an asset to the group. Her background includes rebuilding a tractor, being a bully and putting her victims in cornfields overnight. Penny does display some stereotypes but we are used to that in Omaha.

These aren't the only characters in Omaha, Omaha is full of them! These characters have entertained or are entertaining millions to this day. From books, to movies to TV, Omaha continues to permeate American culture at all levels. Stay tuned!

6
Introduction – Sports

It is a city of fans and spectators of a myriad of amateur sports especially at the collegiate level but Omaha doesn't have a Major League professional team in any sport. No NFL team, no Major League Baseball, no hockey team and Omaha's only brush with the NBA ended in 1979 when the Kansas City/Omaha Kings gave up on the Omaha market. While the franchises may not have a home in the "Big O", the city has been the home and training ground of many great athletes over the years.

Bob Gibson started his professional career as a member of the famous Harlem Globetrotters, handing many a defeat to the Washington Generals. His roommate was Globetrotter legend Meadowlark Lemon. He ended his career as the Hall of Fame pitcher for the St. Louis Cardinals. Gibson is joined in Cooperstown by another Omaha product, longtime Red Sox third baseman, Wade Boggs. Between them they hold 3 World Series Titles, 11 Gold Gloves, 8 Silver Slugger Awards, 5 American League Batting Titles, 21 All-Star teams, an NL MVP Award and various other accolades.

Over the past 60 years or so, Omaha has hosted and witnessed legions of baseball players play their way to titles and the major leagues. The College World Series has captured the collective heart of Omaha as year after year the best collegiate baseball players find glory on an Omaha ball field. College athletics have been the lifeblood of the Omaha sporting world with two universities. Creighton University has been a Cinderella dancing in the March tournament and UNO was the home to a wrestling dynasty winning championships to the bitter end.

Superior college athletes have first made their way through youth and high school athletics here in Omaha. Their hard work and personal development helped propel them into the world of big-time college football. Maybe it was barrier breaking, African-American quarterback Marlin Briscoe who played at the University of Nebraska at Omaha and later became the NFL's first black quarterback. The dream to become the best college football player in the country was motivation for others like Nile Kinnick, Johnny Rodgers and Eric Crouch. Their exploits have given Omaha and the "402," area code the most Heisman Trophy winners of any city in the country. All were committed to excellence and motivated to be champions.

"Bud" Crawford is a World Champion boxer who has taken all comers. His recent fights are part of the fabric of Omaha boxing history. Max Baer became the first Omaha heavyweight to win the boxing crown, only to lose famously to "Cinderella Man," James Braddock. An episode out of that history includes tales of the "Bluffs Butcher" Ron Stander and his fabled challenge to another great boxer, Joe Frazier. Four Rounds of fury…and blood, but Stander remained standing, as a legend for decades now. It is hard to believe that the episode was not in some small way, inspiration for Rocky. Many believe the real inspiration for Stallone's boxing epic was a later Muhammed Ali fight. Perhaps, but the legendary Ali persona was cut from a pattern created in Omaha.

Ali is said to have built his outspoken, acerbic public personality based on the antics of a 1940's and 50's professional wrestler out Omaha. It was Gorgeous George who infuriated audiences with his effete act. He was not alone in Omaha as a legion of wrestlers with their own shtick developed their act in from of Omaha audiences. It is fitting that Omaha was a sort of nexus for professional wrestling to form in the United States. Omaha and Council Bluffs were once the home of Farmer Burn's and his Workout and Wrestling technique.

His mail order technique and the demonstrations he performed around the country accelerated American professional wrestling. His protégés like Frank Gotch are now professional wrestling legends. Omaha has produced a number of superstar professionals through the ages including Ted Dibiase and "Sting." As long as the sport remains popular, Omaha will offer its share.

Omaha has been a part of Professional Sports even when they were not represented. Peyton Manning used Omaha as a code. The legend of Super Bowl champion Steve Young began over a century before his victory in a cottonwood building in Council Bluffs. Stan Bahnsen and Jon Lieber both pitched their way from Council Bluffs throughout Major League Baseball. They started their amateur lives in the metro.

Amateur is the key word for Omaha sports. Perhaps the greatest and most American of stories it that of Johnny Goodman. The South Omaha orphan who went to work on a golf course, learned the game and excelled to the point of becoming the US Open champion. The last amateur to actually win the event. All the while scraping to survive, borrowing clubs and depending on others to loan him clothes for events, Johnny never played for fortune, only for self-edification.

Over the past 160 or so years, Omaha has become a bastion of the quintessential American sports story of athletes who would rise up and defeat the odds. Whether it was conquering poverty, demons, or just the opposition. The sons and daughters of Omaha continue to prove that Omaha is America's Hometown!

Brigham Young's Super Bowl Dreams

Many people in Omaha know the story of Peyton Manning and his "Omaha!" audible during his Super Bowl appearances with the Denver Broncos. What you may not have known is the Omaha connection to the Super Bowl XXIX victory of the San Francisco 49ers.

The story started in Council Bluffs, IA in December of 1847, Joseph Smith, the original prophet of the Church of Latter Day Saints had been murdered over three years prior and the large congregation had sought out new leadership. After several schisms in the church, Brigham Young, the President of the Quorum of Twelve, emerged as the best and most able leader to move the church forward. To that end, in hastily built, cottonwood meeting house, Young was sustained as the President and Second Prophet of the Church of Latter Day Saints.

One of his first major changes to church doctrine was to allow plural marriage. The change was meant to increase the population of the Mormon faith as rapidly as possible. While disdainful today, the switch to plural marriage created dramatic and long-lasting results. Brigham Young himself, married at least 20 women, 16 of whom bore him 57 children. These 57 children bore grandchildren and they have created an Abrahamic level of lineage.

One of his Great, Great Great Grandchildren grew up to play at the University named for his famous Grandfather and often colloquially called, BYU. This man was Steve Young who rose up from the 8th String Quarterback at BYU to become a starter, He would later sign the largest sports contract ever at the time when he first agreed to play for the USFL Las Angeles Express. After the league folded, Young sallied forth into the NFL and eventually found his way into a backup position behind legendary Quarterback Joe Montana. Young patiently waited and finally in 1992, he was given the opportunity to lead the team as Montana recovered from injury.

Young made the best of a tenuous hold on the starting job by turning in a NFL MVP season. The next year, Joe Montana was traded to the Kansas City Chiefs, giving Steve Young the undisputed starting role. The 1994 season saw Steve Young perform at an MVP level once again and take the 49ers to the Super Bowl where they triumphed over the San Diego Chargers.

And it never would have happened had Steve Young's Great-Great-Great Grandfather failed in gaining control of the church and it would have never happened without Plural marriage. All of which happened right here in the Omaha metro!

Farmer Burns and the Rise of Professional Wrestling in America

It seems all children have dreamt of one day entering the squared circle to face off against a villain named "The Animal," or developing their own submission hold they call the "headsplitter." Some of those kids keep that dream and become amateur wrestlers and upon graduating the sport, rummage through, mixing and matching their old Halloween costumes until they come up with something of a superhero alter ego. They find a trainer and enter the world of professional wrestling. Omaha has had several notable professional wrestlers.

Iowa has long been a hotbed, a kind of Mecca for wrestling and this is not one of god's mistakes but rather the life's work of one man. Martin "Farmer" Burns did not create wrestling, nor did he invent the style he popularized. What he did do was to combine a culture of athleticism and physical fitness with his sport.

Burns catch wrestling style is very similar to the modern wrestling we can watch today at the high school and collegiate levels, which in turn is the basis of the type of entertainment we watch in the WWE and other professional wrestling companies. This style of wrestling also is a component of successful MMA fighting styles.

The key to the Burn's technique was to develop the body through simple exercises, stretching and light dumbbell work. In reality, the workout looked less like a program to create the hulking bodybuilder physique of the modern professional wrestler and more like a workout of gymnast. Burns implemented exercises and workout techniques like breathing techniques which are consistent with Judo and Asian martial arts. Burns also added isometrics, calesthenics and footwork drills in lieu of weightlifting. These activities actually promoted the well-being and health of anyone who sought to be healthier, rather than simply wrestlers. The techniques were often copied and carried into other sports.

It is said that Martin Burns competed in over 6000 matches but lost only six. He was at one time the Heavyweight Champion of the World. An amazing feat when we consider that Burns was only 5'9" and 175 pounds. All of this competition gave Burns the opportunity to find great talent to train and mentor in the "Great American Martial Art." Perhaps the greatest talent was Frank Gotch. Frank was a student of Farmer Burns and a contemporary. Frank won the Championship of the world and held the title for almost 7 years. Only a couple of other wrestlers in the history of professional wrestling have had a longer championship reign.

After Burns retired from competitive wrestling, he continued to train wrestlers and promote physical fitness. He moved to Omaha and opened a gym. He also started a newsletter which explained his techniques and exercise philosophies. His methods were sent to thousands of homes which promoted the sport and physical fitness throughout the United States.

Martin "Farmer" Burns helped revitalize and popularize the sport of wrestling and lived long enough to see it disseminated throughout America. It was the very beginning of what we know of as modern professional wrestling. Omaha was a great benefactor of this sport. Omaha became one of the regional powerhouses of professional wrestling. The Dusek family ran the local franchise and were lucky enough to find amazing talent in the area. Omaha produce Baron Von Raschke delighted and terrified crowds with his Claw hold, the Nazi sympathizer Karl Von Hess delighted in the hissing and the boos of the audience, Mad Dog Vachon thrived in Omaha, retired in Omaha, and lived out his life in Omaha. Gorgeous George created modern showmanship that is so much a part of modern professional wrestling. Ted "the Million Dollar Man," DiBiase and Omaha native Sting round out the talent the city has supplied and likely some kid learning the sport in his backyard or in some club will someday crush his mother by becoming a Professional wrestler. Farmer Burns and his Catch Wrestling gave Omaha a legacy as the birthplace of modern professional wrestling.

    Professional Wrestling is a particularly American art form, it makes sense that it would trace its beginnings to America's Hometown!

Gorgeous George Creates Muhammad Ali

Gorgeous George was one of many great wrestlers to have called Omaha home at one point or another. Gorgeous George found his shtick the day one young woman in the audience called him gorgeous, referring to the long curly blonde hair he had. George saw an opening and played on social morays of the 1940's. He did it extravagantly by wearing elegant robes and acting overly effeminate, feeding off the jeering of the crowds.

Playing to the crowds by an athlete had never been done before and George looked for even more ways to build on this new act. He would spray down the ring announcer with perfume to sterilize him. He would wear satin and sequined robes to insinuate that he was homosexual. He had a valet he called Jeffries that would carry perfume and gold plated bobby pins to disinfect the ring and the pins he threw to the fans.

His grand showmanship and flamboyant act came at the very beginnings of television and viewers were buying televisions just to see Gorgeous George and his over the top style. Although it was an act and wrestling by this time was a stage production, viewers were drawn to his ability to excite the crowd and build a popular audience whether it is due to love or hate. A young boxer from Louisville, Kentucky saw the act of Gorgeous George and modeled his persona to match. He even admitted that his poetic riffs and offbeat actions in hyping his first heavyweight title match against Sonny Liston was in emulation of Gorgeous George.

After that bout, and after Muhammad Ali became champion of the world, Gorgeous George went backstage and gave Ali this bit of advice, ""A lot of people will pay to see someone shut your mouth. So keep on bragging, keep on sassing and always be outrageous."

The Godfather of Soul, James Brown, also admitted that he borrowed from the Gorgeous George to create his stage presence. These two are certainly not the only sports heroes to play to the crowd this way. In the 1970's, NFL Quarterback Joe Namath brought attention as he wore a fur coat on the sidelines with fur an exaggerated length. Many Rockstars of the 1970's and 1980's attracted their following wearing glam clothing and makeup often expressing androgynous mannerisms.

In the 1990's we had Dennis Rodman who spent much of the 1980's as an above average basketball player that most people did not know. Dye your hair extreme colors, wear women's clothes and act effeminate on camera? Instant Superstar.

Would "Rocky," be an Oscar winner if we did not have Apollo Creed to hate? Gorgeous George created a way to communicate with the audience and to make them feel one way or another about the act. George Raymond Wagner died at 48 years old of a heart attack but no one will ever forget the role he has made in American culture and in the history of Omaha. The Ali persona, just another piece of the legacy of America's Hometown.

Smokin Joe and The Butcher

Success is not always instantaneous and at times our actions seem like failure. They become a success with the passing of time. On May 25th, 1972, Council Bluffs native, Ron Stander and World Heavyweight Champion Joe Frazier squared off in the only Heavyweight title fight ever to be held in Omaha, NE. For Ron Stander it was the fight of a lifetime against a man who had beaten Muhammad Ali just a year earlier.

The 1970's was known as the Golden Age of Heavyweights. The decade saw the return of Ali, the rise of Joe Frazier, Ken Norton, George Foreman, Earnie Shavers, and George Chuvalo. The battles that defined the Heavyweight ranks of the 1970's were fought all over the United States and all over the world. So in May 1972 the champion of the word, Joe Frazier flew to Omaha, Nebraska, to give a local underdog fighter an opportunity. A snow-white underdog, and put his face on a poster next to his. Frazier was about give a local Council Bluffs boy a shot at the greatest title in the world!

While "The Bluffs Butcher," as Stander was called in the ring, did not have the resume of Joe Frazier, he had beaten the hard punching Earnie Shavers and racked up a strong professional record in the lead-up to the fight. Stander never approached his sport like an elite athlete and instead like a hard punching good-old-boy. His regimen included less road work and raw eggs, and more late night parties and cold beers. Frazier was a chiseled athlete trained who approached all fights with the zeal of a businessman.

The Butcher was an obscure boxer, a "ham and egger," to use a boxing colloquialism. What he did have was a withering right hand and a desire to make his community proud. Most people didn't give him much of a chance. His wife at the time was famously quoted as quipping, "You don't take a Volkswagen into the Indy 500, unless you know of a hell of a shortcut." As he stepped in the ring against the World Champion in his quest to shock the world, the majority of the 10,000 spectators wanted to believe in Ron Stander. He bounded into the ring in red and white trunks, bouncing and shadow boozing for the crowd.

As the fight began, the Butcher worked inside and stayed tight to Frazier, doing what he could to dampen the raw power of "Smokin Joe." Big Ron landed some punches early that stunned Frazier but it wasn't enough. It wasn't long before Frazier opened up cuts around the eyes of Stander. For Stander, it was a problem he contended with throughout his career. By the fourth round, Stander's face was cut in four places and his right eye was closing. His corner knew that it if he did not land that big right hand soon and drop Frazier the night would be over.

Stander came out of his corner like a bull. Frazier dispatched the attacks like a picador doing away with the exhausted bull. Stander continued to swing blindly as the blood flowed into his eyes from the numerous cuts he sustained. Big Ron's face looked like it had been butchered by the end of round four. Before round five, the ring doctor felt like Stander had sustained enough damage and stopped the fight.

There would be no big right hand that would shock the world this night. Joe Frazier, the 10-1 odds on favorite did exactly what was expected of him and ended the hopes and dreams of boxing fans in the Metro. Frazier praised the talent and courage of Stander during the fight and made platitudes that if Stander got the practice and the work he needed that he might warrant a re-match. No re-match was ever scheduled. Frazier instead went on to fight George Foreman who challenged him the night of the Ron Stander fight.

Stander continued to box for another decade, fighting Ken Norton along the way. The Butcher would again be stopped in the 5th Round by Technical Knock-Out. Stander never again found himself in a championship bout. He quietly retired after fighting a series of regional matches with mixed success. Neither Nebraska, nor Iowa has had another Heavyweight contender since that May night in 1972.

Stander continues to reside in the Omaha area and remains active in the boxing community. While Stander may not have won a championship his courage and willingness to face a difficult challenge may have inspired the future. For one evening in 1972, Ron Stander made the world focus on Omaha and watch one of their own in the sport of boxing. Perhaps it prepared Omaha for the future.

Omaha now has a champion of its own in Terence "Bud" Crawford. Crawford unified all of the light welterweight titles and has held his titles since 2013. Crawford has amassed a fine career and is in rarified air, the boxing game in not what it used to be and when he wins, while certainly no dispute regarding his personal greatness, he has not reached the legendary status that Omaha was able to grasp for one night in 1972, during the Golden Age of Heavyweights. A local boy reached for the stars, right here at home, in America's Hometown.

15 Rounds with the Dancing Baer

Max Baer may be a name forgotten by many people today, but in the early 1930's he was the Boxing Heavyweight Champion of the World, This was at a time when boxing was perhaps only surpassed by baseball as the most popular sport in America. A portion of his story was portrayed in the 2005 motion picture "Cinderella Man." What crowds saw in Cinderella Man didn't tell the whole story and didn't really tell about the person he really was.

Baer was born in Omaha, NE to a poor hog farmer. Children of poor hog farmers that grew up in the early 1900's often have a similar story. The family was broke so he dropped out of school in the 8th grade to help on the farm. What he missed in learning he gained in strength and power. As a young man he learned that he had a very powerful right hand, a lesson learned during a moment of youthful capriciousness. He and a group of buddies decided to rob a bar of a jug of wine. When the large proprietor bounded after them, Max turned and knocked him out with a single punch. It was then that Max realized he could become a boxer.

Max fought his first fight in 1929 and quickly rose up the ranks on the power of his right hand. In 1930 he caught his first real break. He fought for the title of Pacific Coast Champion against Frankie Campbell. The power of Baer's right hand did not bring glory. For Max, it brought misery. In the 5th round, Max sensed he was falling behind. With a sense of urgency and a growing rage at the goading of a former friend now in Campbell's corner, he furiously pummeled Campbell against the rope until his opponent collapsed to the floor. Everyone watching knew something was wrong. Max waited by his fallen opponent's side for 30 minutes waiting for the ambulance to arrive. He then followed him to the hospital and waited by his side until the doctors came and notified all involved that Frankie Campbell had died. Max Baer sobbed uncontrollably and apologized profusely to his opponent's widow for his deed.

Baer was charged with manslaughter over this fight. Although the charges were eventually dropped, Frankie Campbell's death in the ring had a profound effect on Baer. The media dubbed him a killer and used this to help market his next fight against Ernie Schaff. Despite having lost to Schaff a year earlier, Baer launched a savage attack and knocked Schaff out completely. While Schaff was revived and left the ring seemingly ok. During his next fight with Primo Carnera, a single jab dropped Schaff and he died in the ring. This sequence of events was blamed on Baer once again. Baer considered retirement forever but was taken under the wing of former champion, Jack Dempsey.

In 1933, Baer was back on the rise. It was also a time when he began to recognize his heritage. In 1933 Max fought Max Schmelling the pride of Nazi Germany. Baer had never really considered his ethnic heritage before and he was not particularly religious but the fact was his father was half Jewish. This made Max a quarter Jewish. His manager used it as a motivational tool, pushing the mantra that Max was fighting against fascism and fighting for the pride of his people. To signify this, he had the Star of David sewn into his trunks. Baer dominated Schmelling throughout the fight before scoring a technical knock out in the 10th round. The victory made Max Baer a hero among American Jews and became a symbol of their fight against German tyranny.

Max would become world champion in 1934 after another technical knockout. This time over the gigantic heavyweight, Primo Carnera. He would hold the championship for 1 year almost to the day. In 1935, Baer would fight James J Braddock. Braddock gained fame with his rags to riches story of triumphing over the tribulations of the depression. So much so that 70 years after the original fight, a motion picture was made about his life and his win over Max Baer for the heavyweight title. The film was not kind to Max Baer and portrayed him as a cold and heartless boxer who was ambivalent over his fight that ended in death. The film also portrayed him as a sort of loutish womanizer. These were unfair portrayals meant to build drama.

According to the people who knew him best, the film was a cartoonish parody of Max Baer. His son stated, "My dad was scatterbrained. He was a bizarre guy, a wonderful guy with kind heart, a great sense of humor and a weakness for the ladies. It's OK to say my dad was a party animal of his era. But he was not the rude, cold-hearted ogre in the movie."

After the loss to Braddock, Baer's heart for boxing weakened both literally and figuratively. He declined as a fighter but continued to fight until 1941. He went back to California to become an actor which was his real passion. After taking a job acting in commercials in 1959, he went to a hotel in Hollywood where he reported that he didn't feel well. The ambulance was called, but Max Baer died on the floor from a massive heart attack.

He left a wife and children which included a son named Max Baer Jr. Max Jr. became a beloved actor in his own right. He played Jethro Bodine in "The Beverly Hillbillies," television program of the 1960's. Max Baer gave Omaha, NE a heavyweight champion and a place in American sports culture. Max Baer is also a hero among American Jews as he is the only Jewish-American Boxer to ever hold a championship belt. Not bad for a hog farmer with an 8th Grade Education. Not bad for the Cinderella City of Omaha…America's Hometown.

Hand the Meatpacker a One Wood!

Cinderella story. Outta, nowhere. A former greenskeeper, now, about to become the Masters champion. It looks like a miracle... It's in the hole! It's in the hole! It's in the hole!
   -Carl Spackler-

It didn't happen exactly like this and it was the US Open and not the Master's but when kids and adults dream of hitting the game winning homerun in the World Series or throwing the touchdown that wins the Superbowl or any other dream of sporting glory, they have a precedent.

One orphan boy from Omaha played his way to the US Open and won. He went on to win the US Amateur title, a feat accomplished by only 11 other golfers in the history of Professional golf in the United States. He sits in rarified air with such greats as Jerome Travers, Chick Evans, Bobby Jones, Francis Ouimet, Goodman, Lawson Little, Arnold Palmer, Gene Littler, Jack Nicklaus, Jerry Pate and Tiger Woods to have won both titles.

Johnny Goodman was one of 10 children of Lithuanian parents who had made South Omaha their home at the turn of the century. The family was impossibly poor making what they could in the packing plants that had drawn them to the city. Johnny's mother tragically died when he was just 10 years old. His father ceased to be a guiding figure and all but abandoned the children to their fate.

Johnny had few options in life at this point. He could beg for work at the meat packing plants or beg. Another option soon came along, but it was in a world that a poor boy could only dream of. Johnny had been taken in by parents of his buddies. As kids of the past used to do, they played outside most of time. They walked the railroad tracks and sought out adventure. One adventure they found just off the tracks was Field Club of Omaha. They watched as men swatted tiny balls with hickory sticks often trailed by boys no older than Johnny and his friends. Goodman set out to become a duffer like the ones he watched.

He soon became a caddie and learned the game of golf. He studiously watched and worked on self-improvement. Golf perhaps matched his quiet and determined behavior, a sport where you may get help here and there on something but largely, you were on your own. Those around him saw his focus and he made friends who looked out for the young orphan boy.

Within three years of becoming a caddie, through myriad pointers and opportunities to caddie with golfing greats; Goodman became a formidable amateur. He borrowed a set of golf clubs in 1925 to enter the Omaha city tournament and at the age of 16 emerged as champion. From here it was all about golf. The day after his big win, Johnny showed his sister the trophy and tried to explain the game. A poor immigrant family in the 1920's could not fathom his fascination with a rich man's game.

In the ensuing years he would travel around the Midwest to golf tournaments. Many times he got there by walking, hitchhiking or stowing away on freight trains. He was still an amateur so winning meant a trophy and glory. He often played in the clothes he wore on the way from Omaha and played with the same worn hickory-sticks that had been handed down to him in the beginning.

His income was itinerant, he worked in print shops or as a messenger boy while finishing high school. Johnny also started following the exploits of another young amateur who became a personal idol, Bobby Jones. In the course of a few years, Johnny took jobs as a caddie or working for the Spalding Company as a clerk but the money he made went to basic survival. So in 1929 when Johnny had an opportunity to go to Pebble Beach, California for the US Amateur tournament, he got community support to travel on a Pullman car. It must have been a far cry from the cattle cars and open freighters he hoboed away just a couple years prior.

Johnny Goodman was about to taste immortality as he matched up against his hero Bobby Jones. The penniless, orphan from Omaha put on a show and narrowly beat Bobby Jones. The win launched him from the ranks of the unknown to a giant in the sport. So many clamored for him to become a pro and make a living at the sport. Goodman wanted to remain an amateur, to play for the love of the game rather than a paycheck. Instead, Goodman became an insurance agent.

In 1933, four years after beating Bobby Jones in California, Johnny Goodman entered the US Open in Chicago. During the open, in a sweltering heat wave, he maintained his lead over the field, besting some of the greatest golfers of the period. He even beat Walter Hagen, the man he had caddied for on the other side of the railroad tracks in Omaha. It is a feat that has still not been replicated some 84 years later.

Jones captured the US Amateur crown once again in 1937 but remained steadfast that he would not become a professional. He continued to scratch out a living, reaching out for his clubs only as an outlet. During the depression work was difficult to come by, it was so bad in fact that Johnny and his wife still could not afford their own home. When the couple finally found the way to build their house, the Japanese attacked Pearl Harbor.

Johnny enlisted and was sent to New Delhi, India. He hated the military but did his duty. In India he grew 4 years older and professional golf started to emerge as a real possibility. He returned home after the war but a short time later, he was driving down an icy road when an animal darted in front of him. He swerved out of control and crashed. He broke his arm in several places and although it mended, Johnny never recovered the elite swing that won him championships in the past.

Johnny finally turned pro in 1950 when he was 41 years old. An age when most modern players may be nearing the end of their career, Johnny made a run at the money. Whatever he did after or whatever he did not achieve can never overshadow the unlikely reality of his life. A young boy, orphaned by his mother and an alcoholic father finds a game beyond his caste and becomes one of its greats.

The rags to riches story permeates American culture. The underprivileged athlete against the rest of the wealthier outside world is also a hallmark of American struggle. Johnny Goodman represent the truth that these are not clichés, but simply possibilities for those captured in desperate situations. Eighty years after his biggest win, Johnny Goodman hasn't been forgotten in Omaha…his hometown. Johnny's feat, representing so much about Americans feel about sports and the possibilities of changing their stars, is what makes Omaha, America's Hometown.

Omaha's New Sheriff?

Omaha does not have an NFL football team. There is no Indoor team, nor a college team in Omaha. The city sates its thirst for gridiron glory through copious amounts of University of Nebraska Cornhusker football. However, Omaha generated a great deal of headlines in the NFL media when a first ballot hall of fame quarterback used our name incessantly on the field. Defenses wanted to know, fans wanted to know, in the end, it isn't clear, except to the inner circle what Peyton Manning meant when he yelled "Omaha," before the snap.

The use of Omaha wasn't new, quarterbacks have used it in the past but never so effectively or prolifically as "The Sheriff." Tom Brady briefly used Omaha before creating his own less awesome cadence. Peyton's little brother Eli used it so much in one game that the defense started to be tipped off as to its meaning. One thing that all of these quarterbacks had in common is that they were using pre-snap calls to give their team instruction. It might be switching a play, a direction or a snap count, it seems every team and every quarterback used their own reference.

Aaron Rodgers, Quarterback of the Green Bay Packers and true Peyton Manning fan summed it up this way. "That's really interesting. The root of that is a timing mechanism where his offense can get off at the same time, and then the beauty and the brilliance of it is that it goes from that word to you saw numerous times he would change it. He would have a code word that would mean it wasn't coming on the 'Omaha.' It wasn't 'Omaha, Omaha, set hut,' that was a dummy." So for Rodgers, it is a dummy call a way to call audible.

Brother Eli of the New York Giants explained, 'Omaha' was in the playbook…There was actually a sheet that said 'Omaha' at the top, and basically 'Omaha' was maybe we change the play, or maybe when I was changing protection, or…the play clock's running down. And 'Omaha' just told everybody to put their hand in the ground, shut up, and the ball's about to be snapped."

Brian Urlacher and Randy Moss explained that it just meant to make the play go in the opposite direction. Invoking the famous "Madden NFL," video game series in his reference, Moss said, "If you've ever played the Madden videogame, "Omaha" is essentially the "flip play" button." To be fair, Madden NFL actually had an "Omaha," call for a couple of years so a player could reverse the play. So Omaha has found its way into the most popular video game series in history without ever fielding an NFL team.

The prevailing theory of Manning's use of Omaha says that the pre-snap call was meant to change the snap count. But this isn't the only reason Manning used it. On many plays the "Omaha" cadence was meant to trick the opposing players into a false start or an "offsides," penalty. This is often referred to a hard count. It is sometimes easier just to ask the man why he yelled Omaha so much.

When asked, Manning explained it clearly and succinctly,

> "I've had a lot of people ask what 'Omaha' means. Omaha is a run play but it could be a pass play, or a play-action pass depending on a couple things — the wind, which way we're going, quarter, and the jerseys that we're wearing. It varies, really play to play. So there's your answer to that one."

If you are still confused, well then the real meaning will probably die with the ages. What is for certain is that one of the greatest quarterbacks in NFL history used Omaha to reach the pinnacle of his sport, winning the Super Bowl twice and racking up unbelievable records. During his run various Omaha organizations supported his efforts and scored their own touchdowns of sorts.

The Greater Omaha Chamber of Commerce recruited 15 area companies to donate $1500 to Peyton Manning's Charitable Foundation, PeyBack, each time he used his Omaha cadence during the AFC Championship game, Super Bowl in 2016. In the end, his group which raises money for disadvantaged children was enriched with a $27, 800 check for all that yelling. The famous Omaha Steaks made their own donation for the Omaha Steaks has confirmed on Twitter that they will be making a $25,000 contribution to All Pro Dad, thanks to Peyton Manning calling "Omaha" out during the big game. Hopefully they sent Peyton a big steak to top off their appreciation.

It wasn't just the city that was excited about the nod from Manning. The original progenitors of the name were proud to see their name repurposed and invited Peyton to visit them where the name actually started. Manning and Omaha ARE "Above all others on the stream!"

Peyton Manning retired after his last Super Bowl victory. At the press conference, he dutifully expressed himself and thanked the fans. He then paid homage to his past coaches and teammates and ended it with a staccato, "So Omaha!"

7
Omaha: The Heart of American Power

Americans are blessed with a certain self-confidence amassed through the development of military power. Prior to World War II, American military power and clout around the world was negligible. Military leaders sometimes sensed the potential power of the United States but overall the world did not see the United States as a real threat militarily. Hitler was often dismissive of the United States as a land of beauty queens and stupid records, but he did respect the industrial possibilities of America. While his ideology clouded so much of his beliefs and his belief that America was a nation of mongrels, he was impressed with the American work ethic and willingness to produce.

Admiral Yamamoto is famously attributed the quote, *"I fear all we have done is to awaken a sleeping giant and fill him with a terrible resolve."* This is actually a quote from the movie Tora! Tora! Tora!. While the quote is quite possibly derived from the mind of Hollywood scriptwriters, it seems this was a general idea that many Japanese leaders felt about American military prowess. After December 7th, 1941, the conjecture faded away as Americans took the field and the formidable industrial might the United States possessed became the Cur that gnashed at the jugular of the axis powers.

Perhaps it was the culture of the city and maybe it was the entrepreneurial spirit the city has always seemed to possess, whatever it was, Omaha helped Uncle Sam roll up his sleeves and show the muscle needed to win the war. Jonathan Browning was the progenitor of American firepower. He was an ingenious gunsmith who answered the call of Joseph Smith to emigrate to the Great Salt Lake. In Council Bluffs, plural marriage became part of the faith of the Latter Day Saints which paved the way for Jonathan Browning to take a second wife. That union produced John Moses Browning. His taught his son his trade and John Moses Browning became a prodigy.

John Moses Browning built the Browning Model 1910, the gun that killed Archduke Franz Ferdinand and embroiled the planet in World War I. The lessons learned throughout WWI and the needs of more powerful weapons to combat armored machines led Browning to go beyond the water-cooled machine guns he made for American use in that war and create a high-caliber, high-firepower weapon. This became the M2 or the "Ma Deuce." The Ma Deuce was the most prolific heavy machine gun of WWII. It was placed in almost every airplane the US produced, from bombers to fighters. The Ma Deuce was mounted on tanks, ships and various vehicles. The M2 was particularly hated by the German military due to the firepower and the modified usage that American forces found to protect themselves with the weapon.

Guns were not the only thing that Omaha gave to the war effort. Andrew Jackson Higgins learned to fight ostensibly at Creighton Prep High School in downtown Omaha. Higgins was expelled for brawling with other students. This may have been an omen as Higgins joined the Army National Guard where he was learned boat building and water navigation. By the start of WWII, he was in dire straits economically. He built a landing craft that became integral for the war in the Pacific and eventually the massive D-Day invasion. Adolph Hitler despised Higgins and called him the "New Noah." Dwight Eisenhower called his invention the boat that won the war.

The planes that ended the war flew out of Omaha as well. The Martin Bomber Plant at Ft. Crook Field in Bellevue, Nebraska built several types of bomber but near the end they were building the Very Heavy B-29 bomber with special bomb carriages. The special order planes were built to carry atomic weapons. The first weapons of their type ever produced were carried by the Enola Gay and Bockscar, two Stratofortress planes pulled off the line in Bellevue. They were sent to Tinian in the Pacific in preparation for the effort to end the war. All of the 8 planes used in the bombings and as escorts came out of the Glenn Martin Bomber plant. Peter Kiewit Construction built the factory, then built the mines that produced the ore for the bomb casings. Omaha fingerprints were all over the bombings of Hiroshima and Nagasaki.

After the war, the Storz family took the lead in landing the Strategic Air Command base here in Omaha. With this success came the presence of Curtis Lemay, the general who had commanded the attacks on Hiroshima and Nagasaki, the father of the modern Air Force came to Omaha to build a modern Nuclear Air Force. It seemed fitting since Omaha had been the city where American military aviation began and had been home of the first American aviator and pilot.

American power around the world stemmed from our success in WWII. Omaha, Nebraska had a strong hand in that success and continued to contribute to United States safety and interests throughout the cold war. When the Cold War shift from earth to the Space Race, Omaha put their foot in to insure success. Dehner Boots shod the astronauts that America sent to space. At every turn, Omaha was there to offer their talents and abilities to make sure America was strong. The American people were able to grow and excel with the knowledge that they and their families were safe from the outside world and American interests were in good, strong, hands.

To forget the regular soldiers, sailors and members of the air corps who fought for American freedom in any war would be a sin. Whether they were from Omaha, or any other city in the country, their efforts on behalf of their nation and their fellow citizens in not in vain. Omaha is America's Hometown so our heroes are always welcome!

Browning: Clinging to Guns and Religion

What is a Mormon? Where do Mormons live? How can I tell what a Mormon looks like? Does he carry a big machine gun? Some people have never had any real connection with Mormons, or more appropriately Latter Day Saints. Their only experiences may be from stereotypical images provided by TV shows and Broadway musicals. One of the questions was kind of random. Do Mormons carry big machine guns? The answer would be occasionally and a follow up question might be do Mormons build big machine guns. The answer would be at least one very talented family does. The family patriarch spent time in the metro area and from his skills grew an industry that has helped the United States become and remain the world's only superpower.

Jonathan Browning was born in Tennessee but as was customary at the time, moved with the frontier. In the 1830's he was an expert gunmaker, living in Quincy, Illinois. In 1838, Browning first came in contact with the Mormons as they were being forcefully expelled from Missouri. During the same period, Browning invented the "Harmonica Gun," this was the first real innovation in the development of semi-automatic and eventually fully automatic weapons. It was a breech-loading handgun with a clip that loaded in the side of the weapon, feeding ammunition from a cartridge that moved from right to left rather than modern weapon clips that feed the chamber from the bottom.

Browning's gun made him a well-known gunsmith in the area and his weapons commanded a high price. This changed in 1842 when Browning met the Latter Day Prophet Joseph Smith. From the power of this meeting, Jonathan Browning converted and became a Latter Day Saint. His conversion came at a high personal cost as the local denizens of Quincy turned on Browning. Those who had once been friendly or were past customers treated him as a pariah. Browning sold his Quincy gun shop and moved to Nauvoo with the rest of the saints.

Peace did not follow Browning to Nauvoo. The people of Illinois were generally hostile to the Latter Day Saints and in 1844, a mob in Carthage, Illinois formed at the jail where Joseph Smith and his brother Hyrum were being held. After a shootout, Joseph Smith was shot several times and died after falling out of a tall window. Persecution continued until Brigham Young led the Saints from Nauvoo and across Iowa.

The Mormons arrived in modern day Council Bluffs, Iowa in 1846 and almost immediately the US Government came to raise a Mormon Brigade. Jonathan Browning originally volunteer for service but Brigham Young the interim leader of the church convinced him that his skills as a gunsmith were needed in the Grand Encampment of the Saints in Council Bluffs. Browning stayed and soon put out his shingle as a gunsmith. An old advertisement published in a Mormon publication entitled the *Frontier Guardian*, was published in Council Bluffs, Iowa, and noted his entry into business:

> GUNSMITHING. The subscriber is prepared to manufacture, to order, improved Fire-arms, viz: revolving rifles and pistols; also slide guns, from 5 to 25 shooters. All on an improved plan, and he thinks not equalled this far east. (Farther west they might be.) The emigrating and sporting community are invited to call and examine Browning's improved fire-arms before purchasing elsewhere. Shop eight miles south of Kanesville on Musquito Creek, half a mile south of Trading Point. JONATHAN BROWNING.

The move to Council Bluffs was not only a change in geography but of social and political change among the Saints. In 1847, Brigham Young was voted as the second president of the Church of Jesus Christ of Latter Day Saints. This was extremely important to the future of the saints and what would happen with Jonathan Browning specifically. While the concept of plural marriage was probably enacted and promoted by Joseph Smith in Nauvoo, after the election of Brigham Young, it became open practice in Council Bluffs.

Plural families became freely acknowledged and the practice spread among the Mormons. This allowed Jonathan Browning to take three wives. His second wife gave birth to 3 children, one of them a boy named John Moses Browning. Jonathan taught his son Jonathan Moses everything about gun manufacturing. By the time Jonathan Moses was 13, he was building guns in his father's shop, by the time he was 24, he was patenting new weapons. His first patent was the 1885 Winchester Single Shot Rifle, which is still being produced today.

From this early start, Jonathan Moses Browning went on to a long career of weapon innovation and invention which included the Browning 1910 Colt, which was the gun that killed Archduke Franz Ferdinand and started World War I. He also was the innovator of the Browning Automatic Rifle, the first widely used American light machine gun. The BAR as it became known, was used throughout WWII all the way until the early part of the Vietnam conflict. The BAR was so reliable that it was much more popular than the early versions of the Armalite M-16 which was meant to replace the BAR.

For the average man, Browning invented the pump shotgun and later the semi-automatic shotgun. Browning also invented the over-under shotgun which proved to be a much more accurate weapon, a useful innovation for bird hunting. Over-Under shotguns are also the weapon of choice for competition skeet shooters.

Perhaps Browning's most important contributions were those weapons he created for military service. The M1911 was designed for its high powered .45 cartridge. The power and reliability of the weapon made it the preferred sidearm of the armed services from pre-WWI through the Vietnam Conflict. While it has been surpassed in use in modern times by the 9mm M9 Beretta, some officers still prefer and still carry M1911 Brownings.

Of all the weapons that Browning produced, perhaps his most important innovation was the M2 Browning. This weapon may possibly be the most important weapon in US military history. It was designed during the waning years of WWI and is still in production today which has made it the longest produced machine gun in history. The M2, referred to as the "Ma Deuce," by those who have used the weapon quickly became a favorite of the US Military. The M2 proved to be an incredibly versatile and powerful weapon that was used in several phases of the war. Its cartridge had 4 times more power than the average rifle which meant that it could pierce inch thick armor and is lethal at over a mile away. This means it was effective against armored vehicles, airplanes, personnel and a variety of other military targets.

Most of the airplanes produced in WWII were equipped with M2s including the P-40, P-47, and P-51's. This means that the famous Flying Tiger's with their iconic shark face logo, used the P-40 and consequently the M2 as their weapon of choice. The Red Tailed Tuskegee Airmen protected their bombers with the M2. B-17's were possibly the most widely used bomber of WWII. The very famous "Memphis Belle," was a B-17 and it was protected with 13 M2 .50 Machine guns, located strategically on the plane.

Jonathan Moses Browning created some of the most enduring designs in history. The M2 is nearly 100 years old and is still in widespread use throughout the world and in the United States Military. American snipers still consistently use weapons that use the .50 Browning cartridge for impressive results. Famed American Sniper Carlos Hathcock used a .50 BMG to set the longest sniper kill in history which stood from 1968 until 2009. Hathcock was a remarkable sniper using a remarkable weapon.

      John Moses Browning is considered the greatest weapons designer in history. He did most of his work in the same old shop near Ogden, Utah, left to him by his father Jonathan Browning. Jonathan Moses would never have been born had the elder not joined the Mormon Church and travelled to Council Bluffs, Iowa where plural marriage was first openly practiced. It was his father's skills that Jonathan Moses Browning was able to learn and add to in his incredible life of weapons innovation which included the machine gun that has helped us remain the world's superpower and continues to keep America safe to this day.

Top Gun for Blimps

"I feel the need...the need to float and be propelled forward at a fairly low speed!" The line just doesn't quite sound the same as the famous line from Top Gun. Then again, military aviation has made leaps and bounds over the past 100 years. While Kitty Hawk may have been the birthplace of flight, Nebraska was where early fliers came to learn the craft. For example, legendary aviator Charles Lindbergh learned to fly in Lincoln.

Omaha, Nebraska even had their own airplane manufacturer, the Roos-Bellanca Airplane Company was formed in 1921. The company produced a single unit of a plane that was very advanced for its time. . It was one of the first enclosed cockpit planes which made it far more practical. Unfortunately, the company formed and produced their product before Air Mail services really gained traction and made airplane production a profitable enterprise.

The military identified an interest in aviation in all of its forms very early in development. The French developed the hot air balloon for military reconnaissance in the late 1700's but the United States chose to adopt the advancement during the 1860's. The army operated a balloon corps during the first few years of the Civil War. After a review of the program in 1863, the balloon program as it had been first organized, was disbanded. Although, there was no official aerial warfare campaign after 1863, the military remained interested in the concept.

Early balloons were too small and the technology to rudimentary to carry ordinance but as explosive technology became lighter and more compact, lighter than air craft became a much more viable military option. New technologies developed in Europe created larger and more stable balloons. The United States became reinvigorated in their interest of lighter than air craft during the Spanish-American War. During the battle for Cuba, a balloon was used to identify troop movements on San Juan Hill. The mitigated success of this action moved the US Army to re-introduce a permanent ballooning program after the war.

As school was first started in Virginia after the war but in 1905 was transferred to Fort Omaha. In 1907, the Aeronautical Division of the US Army Signal Corps was developed. This was the original pre-cursor to the United States Air Force. The new division under the command of Captain Charles deForest Chandler quickly identified new innovations through use of air power. Lieutenant Frank Purdy Lahm would join the division soon after. Lahm and Chandler were both trained in ballooning. Lahm for his part had just won the Gordon Bennett Cup, which was the first balloon racing event ever held, an event that continues to this day.

In 1908, Wilbur and Orville Wright proved their concept of heavier than air craft and the military immediately sent the brothers an order for a plane, the Signal Corps also purchased dirigibles to be placed into service. By 1909, Frank Lahm was trained in flying both rigid and non-rigid dirigibles as well as the airplane. This made Lahm, America's first aviator. In 1962, Curtis LeMay honored Lahm with a citation noting him as the first military aviator. Because of the fact that he spent nearly his entire military career learning aviation skills, he is also known as the father of Air Force flight training.

During WWI, as it became evident that observation balloons and aerial navigation was key to battlefield success. The Fort Omaha Balloon School cranked out trained balloonists, ready for the battlefields of France. Omaha did everything it could during WWI. In fact, the city of second in the nation in per capita enlistments during the war. WWI was also the first war where airplanes were used to fight. Dogfighting between planes was born and Omaha had a connection to this as well. The first commanding officer of the Balloon School, Charles deForest Chandler proved that a machine gun could be fired from an airplane.

Fort Omaha continued to organize Balloon companies throughout the war. In all, 13 balloon companies were trained and sent to Europe where they distinguished themselves. Veterans who survived the war organized reunions to visit Omaha for years afterward. American military aviation rose quickly from almost nothing. An army that went from horse cavalry charges to the cutting edge of aeronautics technology. They flowed from Omaha, America's first Top Gun!

First in War, First in Peace

In August 1945, WWII had dragged on between the United States and the Empire of Japan for four long years. America had not yet become the economic superpower she aspired to be and the nation was weary of war, both economically and spiritually. Japan was losing, but anticipation mounted as the Marines island-hopped to the doorstep of the main islands of Japan.

In the United States, the military had assembled a team of genius engineers to build a bold new weapon. Planes were developed to deliver the new weapon. With the anxiety over the toll a conventional invasion of Japan might take on our military, the only question left was if the weapon would be delivered. In the late June and early July, President Harry Truman made the decision to use , "the most terrible bomb in the history of the world…" against Japan. On August 6th and again on August 9th,1945, the bombs were delivered. They were the final daggers in the heart of Japan.

After the battle of Leyte Gulf in 1944, the Imperial Japanese Navy was shattered. The loss of the Philippines separated from territories they occupied in the South Pacific, places that furnished the Japanese empire with oil, rubber and other war materials. Without aircraft carriers and their forces devastated, the most powerful part of the Japanese military power was left unable to conduct major operations.

The Japanese Army suffered an almost unbroken string of defeats over the previous two years. The Americans had taken Okinawa in July 1945 and were beginning their planning for the Allied Invasion of the Japanese homeland. With the fall of Germany in Europe, the Russians declared war on Japan and re-deployed military units to the Siberian Border just north of Japanese held Manchuria. The walls were closing in on the Fascist empire and they knew it. When the bombs fell on Japan, the emperor and the high command folded their war efforts and sued for peace.

After weeks of negotiations for cessation of the war, the American military began occupation of Japan on August 28th of 1945, thereby officially ending hostilities. The official ceremony was held on September 2nd, 1945 aboard the American Battleship, USS Missouri. The ceremony was attended by members of all Allied Powers. Vice Admiral John McCain had suffered a series of heart attacks during the war, leaving him frail and weak made his way to Tokyo Bay. His son Lt. Commander John McCain Jr., born in Council Bluffs, IA, sailed his submarine into the bay as well.

On September 2nd, the two witnessed together as the Japanese formally signed the accord and WWII finally ended. It was said that Admiral McCain was a fighting man to the end. With the end of WWII, Admiral McCain Sr., steamed for home. He died four days after the Japanese surrendered on September 6th, 1945. As for John McCain Jr., he became an admiral as well. The only father and son Admirals ever in the United State Navy.

Omaha not only represented in the war and the projection of war around the world, but the Metro also represented the peace as the McCain's watched as the Japanese accepted their defeat. They won the peace and their family legacy has continued to serve the United States and Omaha, America's Hometown.

"New Moses," Insures American Victory

Dec. 7th, 1941 the date that will live in infamy. This is a day that is ingrained in the brains of all Americans as the day the United States entered WWII. Our involvement not only extended to war in the Pacific with Japan, but also against Nazi Germany in Europe.

In Europe, the United States wanted to proceed with an immediate attack on France. The rest of the Allies were convinced that the war effort would be better served with the United States in a supporting role in North Africa. The United States acquiesced and the first American troops went to North Africa. This turned out to be a fortuitous arrangement for the United States as only 9 Months after its entry into the war, the Allied forces launched an amphibious invasion of the Port of Dieppe in Northern France with disastrous results.

The failure at Dieppe taught the allies a number of lessons. Primarily they needed to have an overwhelming force and they needed in-depth planning. In 1942, the war was still very much in doubt, in fact the Germans had little to be concerned with in Europe. They controlled most of Western Europe and developed what Hitler referred to as his "Atlantic Wall. The wall was an extensive system of defenses and fortifications built along the coastlines of the countries Germany occupied. The system made launching an ordinary attack on the mainland of Europe a formidable task.

This was an important issue because without an Allied advance on the mainland, the Germans could focus their efforts on the Eastern fronts where they were concerned with defeating the Russian Army. Germany was facing their own problems in the Soviet Union and the Russians were slowly recapturing territory lost to the Germans. This created concerns in allied quarters that would come to a head later.

Plans for a large scale Allied assault somewhere in Mainland Europe began in earnest in 1943 as American forces gained battlefield experience in North Africa and Italy. It was clear this experience was important as the first American performances were rather lackluster when fighting against forces that were inferior to those they would face elsewhere on the continent. In the meantime, in the United States, a man was building boats, lots of boats.

Andrew Jackson Higgins was a failed lumberman and shipper before WWII. He was attempting to become a shipbuilder during the depression, some say his efforts to build boats were to assist bootleggers with shipping their Caribbean based cargo. The need for boat builders at the outbreak of WWII was fortuitous for Higgins and his efforts were advantageous to the war effort.

Higgins learned the basics of boat building and navigation on the Platte River after joining the Army National Guard. He learned to fight even before that. Andrew Jackson Higgins was a student at Creighton Prep in Omaha before being expelled for fighting. Higgins found his way to the Gulf Coast of the United States and worked in various trades which required him to learn to navigate the bayous and coastal bodies of water found in the area. When WWII ramped up, these learned skills would be important.

The US military needed boats that would allow them to launch amphibious attacks in Europe, since they did not have a place to launch attacks and in the Pacific theatre because they were moving from island to island in the South Pacific, harassing the Japanese Imperial Army. Higgins developed a boat called the "Eureka Boat," the US Marine Corp was not satisfied with their existing options in moving troops to shore and so considered the Eureka Boat for this duty. Initial testing found that the Higgins boat exceeded the performance of anything the Navy was using at the time. The design was modified to change the front wall of the landing craft into a ramp to unload passengers and equipment.

On Tuesday June 6th 1944, Operation Overlord swept into action. The attack most commonly referred to as D-Day began and it proved to be the finest hour for Andrew Jackson Higgins and his landing craft. The Allied Forces landed 24,000 troops onto the Normandy Coast at just after midnight. By 7 AM they were unloading armored vehicles and other heavy equipment, all from a base of about 2,800 ships. But it was the 4,126 Higgins Boats that ensured success for the allies.

While it was a difficult victories with over 10,000 Allied casualties, the Allies did form a beachhead. How important was this in winning the war? The war had been fought by the majority of the allies since 1939 and the US had entered the war in 1941. So for nearly 5 years, the Allies had fought the Germans to a near stalemate. D-Day ended the struggle and allowed the Allies to progress on the rest of Europe. At the time, the Germans were slowly losing ground to the Russians, who they had focused their greatest efforts on. Had the German army collapsed suddenly on the Eastern front and the Russians were able to advance and take over more ground, with the Allies watching from the sidelines, Mainland Europe may have had to deal with a new dictatorship. After D-Day however, the war was over in less than 1 year, ending in Europe in April 1945.

The land that the Russian Army was able to occupy became the Warsaw Pact which forced millions of Europeans into Soviet Style Communist Economies. The area that the Allies liberated became NATO and were able to make their own choices after the war.

It may be the mundane details that may have become part of the fabric of history. Higgins boats may have been the key to landing on the beach, but there is a further element to the story. D-Day was in planning for over a year. Omar Bradley, was working on the planning from his headquarters in England. When he was first assigned to England, he brought two carpenters to renovate the property. One was Gayle Eyler from Omaha, Nebraska the other was a man from Provo, Utah whose name has been lost to the ages.

Shortly after the two carpenters began work and Bradley started mapping out the attack, Eyler saw the maps with two areas of Normandy beaches named Omaha and Utah. Later Eyler and his partner were in audience when Bradley suggested the names to the Allied Commanders during morning coffee. While it is hard to know how true the story is, whether Bradley was honoring the carpenters or whether the names were chosen by other cosmic forces. Regardless of all other reasons for the city of Omaha being involved in D-Day. She will be forever connected to the history of D-Day and the triumph over Nazi Germany.

The Higgins boat found success in the Pacific theater as well, allowing the Allies to chase the Japanese off many islands of the South Pacific. Higgins Boats were used as the Battles of Guadalcanal, Tarawa, Tinian, Phillipines, Iwo Jima and Okinawa. Perhaps the most important of these battles was the Battle of Tinian. Tinian is a small island in the Marianas Islands. After the capture of Tinian in 1944, the Navy SeaBees build North Airfield which became the busiest airfield in the Pacific. This is the airfield that would be used to launch the Enola Gay and Bockscar on their missions to drop bombs on Hiroshima and Nagasaki.

In the end one of the sons of Omaha made a profound effort to the Allied success in WWII. His ingenuity and perhaps his good luck, gave the military the tool they needed to make inroads into Europe and to defeat the Japanese by hopping from island to island in the Pacific. Higgin's work was so beneficial to the war effort that General Dwight Eisenhower was quoted as saying General Dwight Eisenhower is quoted as saying, "Andrew Higgins ... is the man who won the war for us. ... If Higgins had not designed and built those LCVPs, we never could have landed over an open beach."

Omaha won WWII? There is more evidence to this claim....

We'll Put a Boot in Your Ass, the American Way!

These words famously from a rousing patriotic song from Toby Keith. The song reflects a profound part of American culture; that being that the United States is the world's only superpower. To become a superpower many things must come together and Omaha, Nebraska is a sort of nexus for many seemingly inconsequential things that gave America her status in the world.

Americans have come to expect winning in any conflict they endeavor to face. Toby Keith told the world what we do when you rattle our cage, but in order to stomp our enemies…you gotta have the boots that will do the stomping. So what are the elements that make America a superpower? We have great military leaders, great intelligence, amazing leaders and we are a leader in the exploration of all that surrounds us.

It is often said that it is the shoes that make the man. If that is true, the boots must create the icon. Omaha, Nebraska is the home of one of the last high-end custom bootmakers in the United States. The manufacturer builds them the same way they have for the past 130 years. George S. Patton famed WWII tank commander, rampaged across Europe, conquering over 10,000 Square Miles in 10 days. He saved the 101st Airborne Division, pinned down at the Battle of the Bulge in Belgium…all while trudging through Nazis in a pair of "Tank Boots," that he and the Dehner Boot Company designed together.

Dwight D. Eisenhower wore his Dehner boots as a graduate of West Point. They were the choice of General Omar Bradley, Matthew Abrams and another tank commander Creighton Abrams as they led the American military to victory and excellence. Alexander Haig wore them in the Nixon White House and famously took control of the executive branch in 1981 when President Reagan was shot.

William Westmoreland fought to slow the Domino Theory from engulfing all of Southeast Asia. Norman Schwarzkopf led our troops to victory during the First Gulf War. One of Schwarzkopf's Captains in the Infantry division gradually rose through the ranks to become General HR McMaster, current National Security Advisor for President Donald Trump. All of these men wore Dehner Boots as they guarded the United States and its interests. It isn't just military that makes a country great and we seek to meet the call for any phase that is needed.

On May 1st, 1960, a U-2A spy-plane took off from an airbase in Pakistan with the Mission to photograph the Soviet Union. The U-2 was designed to fly at the edge of the stratosphere, outside the range of surface to air defenses…at least that is what our military intelligence understood at the time. The plane glided over the Ural Mountains in the former Soviet Union, rattling off photos with a state of the art camera that could capture high resolution pictures taken from 70,000 feet. The Russians knew the flight was coming and put all of their defenses in the region on red alert. They also employed a new ultra-high altitude surface to air missile system called the S-75 Dvina. The Russians sent fighter planes to attack Power's plane but they simply couldn't reach the heights of the specially designed craft. The Russians launched fourteen S-75 Dvina Missiles and one of them hit their mark, breaking the plane into pieces.

In the chaos of the moment, Powers could not find the self-destruct button to immolate the plane. He hurtled to the ground and was able to deploy his parachute. His intent was to escape when he landed but the Russians were waiting for him and he was captured immediately.

Gary Powers was quickly charged with espionage by the Russian government and sentences to 3 years imprisonment and 7 years of hard labor. He served two years when in February 1962 the United States and Russian governments agree to exchange prisoners. Gary Powers was released in Potsdam, East Germany where he walked over the Glienicke Bridge to freedom wearing his Dehner Boots.

After the U-2 was knocked down, the United States recognized that their high flyers were also vulnerable and designed the ultra-high speed SR-71 Blackbird. It was the highest-flying and fastest-flying plane during its career. In its 35 years of service the SR-71 collected secret reconnaissance and was never shot down. The flight crews were all wearing Dehner boots.

American greatness is also measured by the bravery of its explorers.

When the United States began the Space Race in the late-1950's and early-1960's. Dehner received boot orders for astronauts in the Mercury program. Then it was the Apollo program. Dehner has built boots for 30 astronauts including Neil Armstrong and "Buzz" Aldrin. While there are no confirmed Dehner boots in space they were certainly used in the NASA program. "Buzz" Aldrin certainly wore Dehner boots at his graduation from West Point.

Strategic Air Command at Offutt Air Force Base in Bellevue, Nebraska was the quintessential symbol of American strength. It's founder was the ultimate cold warrior, Curtis LeMay. He wore Dehner boots and outfitted all SAC Bomber pilots with "Alert," boots. Curtis LeMay wore his boots all the way to the Kennedy White House where he became the Air Force Chief of Staff. In September 1962, LeMay famously clashed with President John F. Kennedy over the management of the Cuban Missile Crisis. All while doffing his custom made Dehner Boots.

On November 22nd, 1963, John F. Kennedy fell to a sniper's bullet in Dallas, TX. His body was flown back to Washington DC for a state funeral planned by his grieving wife Jackie. One of the highlights of his funeral was Black Jack, the riderless horse. The horse was saddled with Dehner boots reversed in the stirrups. Dehner produced these boots at Jackie Kennedy's request in just a few days. Kennedy was not the only president associated with Dehner. If Kennedy was the fighter in the thick of the Cold War, Ronald Reagan was the leader who ended the fight.

He was known as the cowboy. Some of the most beloved images of Ronald Reagan shows him decked out in western wear, working on his ranch. Detractors saw him as a trigger happy cowboy, perpetually on the edge of war with Russia. Like the hero in an old Western, Reagan called the Soviet Union, the Evil Empire and vowed to destroy it.

Dehner doesn't make cowboy boots, they make riding boots and had made boots for Ronald Reagan since the 1930's. In June of 2004, Dehner Boot made President Ronald Reagan one last pair of boots. Boots that were reversed in the stirrups for his funeral procession. One final ride for the man that Americans said was the greatest president ever.

Dehner has connected Omaha to a variety historical events. Their prolific quality and style have made them the choice of military, astronauts and world leaders. They have also found their way into other parts of American Popular culture. American Law Enforcement, especially motorcycle patrols often wear riding boots in their daily work. Dehner has long been a provider for the California Highway Patrol and the Rhode Island State Police. Both of these organizations have been blessed with a television or motion picture counterpart.

Dehner provided patrol boots for the CHiPS TV Program in the late 1970's. Jim Carrey wore Dehner in the 2000 comedy about a deranged Rhode Island State Policeman in *Me, Myself, and Irene.* James Dean and Sylvester Stallone have also made appearances with the Dehner line. The Beach Boys have also been customers of the famous bootmaker

While boots may not be the most important part of American history and culture. Being the best is a powerful part of being American. As Carlton Dehner once explained in this regard, "I've always wanted to put out the best boots in the world, not the most boots." Dehner represents the best. The company links Omaha to a variety of world events and solidifies our position as a world power. Dehner Boots are still proudly, custom-made in Omaha, America's Hometown.

Building America

The American people proved their dynamism and resourcefulness throughout World War II. We sent off our men to war and Rosie the Riveter picked up the slack. We toiled, and we scrimped and we saved, regardless of our role in life. The effort and sacrifice, the blood and tears all reaped rewards as the United States and its allies triumphed over tyranny in WWII.

At the end of WWII, there was one nation that stood, unscarred by the physical wounds of war. The war had accelerated the growth and power to elite status in the world. The United States became a superpower and American interest grew throughout the world. Like the comic books tell us, with great power comes great responsibility. This meant that America had to be everywhere, Leo A Daly Company answered the call and built the facilities that helped the United States weather the Cold War.

Leo A Daly was on hand to design underground missile silos in strategic locations all over the world. The motion picture, "Ice Station Zebra," was based on true events that happened in 1959. Leo Daly had a hand in this as they designed radar stations all over the artic as the United States became ever vigilant in their surveillance of the Russian horizon. Back in Omaha a new headquarters was built at Offutt Air Force Base. The Martin Bomber plant that had birthed thousands of planes for the war effort and created the machines that ended the war was converted into the first command post.

In 1956-57 Leo Daly began work on the "Molehole," the engineering phenomenon that is the hallmark of the cold war. The "Molehole," is an underground command center. It has 24 inch hardened reinforced concrete walls and base floors, 10 inch thick intermediate floors and a 42 inch thick roof and sealed blast-proof doors. The tunnel in and out had 2 foot thick walls and 8 feet in diameter.

The underground center was completed with the best communications equipment of the time. A 16 foot display screen was installed with a number of other screens monitoring a variety of military concerns. Maps of other military installations ran along the length of the concourse. It as if Ian Fleming was consulted to create a secret underground lair. Except, this was pre-Dr. No and it was a serious practical undertaking.

For the majority of the cold war, the "molehole," existed to protect 1000 personnel and to sustain 800 for up to two weeks. With technology advances and changes in the abilities of our enemies, Leo Daly was tapped again to remodel the facility. Between 1986 and 1989, Leo Daly built a 16,000 ft addition and made the complex resistant to Electro-Magnetic Pulse attacks. The new facility was retooled with the latest, greatest communications and computers. All of this was probably necessary, but the military and the government indeed took some of their reasons for revamp from the Hollywood images of what a command center should be. If you are not on the USStratcom high command and cannot tour the molehole. Similar images can be seen in the Tom Clancy films of the late 1980's and 1990's.

It was from the "molehole" that the "Looking Glass," flights were coordinated. The Looking Glass mission was actually a program to mirror the activities of the underground headquarters. The idea is if the ground headquarters was somehow destroyed or cut-off, operations would be mirrored or taken over by the Looking Glass airborne flight which remained perpetually in the sky. It was a peculiar part of the Cold War experience.

The Cold war was an anxious and uncertain time, a time where it seems our military and our government was continually waiting for the proverbial shoe to drop. The United States Air

Force provided the muscle, Leo Daly provided the building knowhow to carry out the mission. Leo Daly did not simply build Offutt's properties but also helped the United States by constructing bases in Vietnam and in other sites around the world.

The company was dedicated to the safety and success of the American military and for the most part they have been an unspoken part of American power. Leo Daly is not a war contractor, they are a world class architecture firm who when asked has answered the call of their nation, but they have also contributed to the glory of winning the peace.

In 1993, nearly 50 years since the hostilities of WWII ended, the United States still had not honored the sacrifice of those who defeated fascism and aggression throughout the world. In the same year, President Bill Clinton signed a law that allowed the American Battle Monuments Commission to build a World War II Memorial in Washington DC. The memorial would honor over 16 million Americans who served their country during WWII and commemorates 405,399 Americans who paid the ultimate sacrifice for Pax Americana. The monument is a piece of American national unity a reminder of what a free people can do when they are dedicated to one national cause.

The majority of the money for the memorial was raised through private donations. Former Senator Bob Dole was the chairman of the fundraising committee and a combat wounded WWII veteran. Academy Award winning actor Tom Hanks lent his credibility and popularity to the project and the goal of $197 Million was achieved to build the monument.

When it came to design the monument, Leo Daly was on hand to create a design team and turn vision into reality. Work on the monument began in 2001 and On May 29, 2004, a four-day "grand reunion" of veterans on the National Mall culminated in the dedication of this tribute to the legacy of "The Greatest Generation." In war and in Peace, the achievements of Leo Daly continue to be remarkable. They have created the utilitarian masterpieces of war that have secured our nation and the beaux-arts and grandeur dedicated to those who united as one nation to win the peace.

8
Odds and Ends

The long history of Omaha is a story full of strange chapters and interesting anecdotes. Omaha's early history ebbed and flowed on the tide of western discovery and exploration. The Mormons really became the first European inhabitants of what would become Omaha. They blazed a path out of a pre-historic trail in the Platte River Road. Their activities would set off a Gold Rush in the late 1840's into the 1850's helping to replenish the population of Council Bluffs as Mormons abandoned the city for their new Zion in Utah. A decade later, a depressed city of Omaha would be revived by a new rush for riches as prospectors fitted out in Omaha for the Colorado Gold fields around a mountain named for explorer Zebulon Pike.

Pike would die during the War of 1812, 40 years before Omaha was founded. The Omaha area, however, would have a hand in the war as Spaniard, Manuel Lisa would be tasked by the United States government to placate the Native Tribes of the Upper Midwest to keep them from joining the war effort in favor of the British. Manuel Lisa became acquainted with and developed close relations with the Omaha Indians, the owners of the area on which the city of Omaha was founded. The Omaha Indians are particularly notable in American history as they were the first Native American masters of the horse. This made them the first full nomadic plains culture, able to follow their main food staple, American Bison.

The Pottawatomi Indians were relocated by the US Government to the Council Bluffs. This gave them control of a marshy, lakeside area known as "Wild Garlic." We know it today as the city of Chicago. Just over a century later, Jewish mobsters would collude to turn a dusty, desert outpost into the world's most well-known resort destination. An Omaha casino mogul would make its number on asset accessible to all Americans.

Moving around the new nation was a part of life in the 1840's. In 1845, as war with Mexico became inevitable, 1000 Mormon men marched out of Council Bluffs and across the United States to play a support role in Southern California. Their major contribution was to create better road systems for the area. Their presence in California was fate. Shortly after the conflict with Mexico, the men travelled north to Sutter's Mill where they helped set off the gold rush. The flood of new emigres and prospectors helped create the cities of Northern California.

As a young city, Omaha and Council Bluffs sent some of their sons and their most prominent citizens to fight in Southern battlefields. Abraham Lincoln visited the area about a year before he became president and set into motion the industry that would dominate Omaha and Council Bluffs over the next century. John Creighton would find Omaha as he worked west to create a nationwide network of instant communications. Lincoln was enamored with the telegraph and when he entered the White House he used new technology to communicate with far off generals. He used the telegraph lines to bind the wounds of war. In 1863, he told his telegraph clerk to tap out a message that freed all slaves in Confederate states, effectively ending American slavery. The clerk would later move to Omaha and start the Omaha Bee. His journalism and viewpoints would help shape the new city for better and for worse. His presence forever linked Omaha to the Emancipation Proclamation and the reclamation of one union.

As Omaha grew and developed a society that included stratification beyond the steely-eyed gamblers and the rugged frontiersman that built the early city. Omaha was able to follow different paths. Oscar Wild passed through both Council Bluffs and Omaha in 1882 and let his feelings be known on the subject of aesthetics. When asked what he thought of Omaha he replied,

> *"You have not the lower orders of the eastern cities. I find less prejudice and more simple and sane people. The western part of America is really the part of the country that interests us in England because it seems to us that it has a civilization that you are making for yourselves — not the complimentary echo of British thought."*

American thought abounds in Omaha. The city has seen the cultures and subcultures form in the face of the broader American culture and watched as they faded into something altogether different. Jack Kerouac rode the rails like a Modernist Hobo as he extolled about the cute little cottages of Council Bluffs and his good fortune in Downtown Omaha as he wended his way cross country to be the founding writer of the "Beat," generation. The "Beatniks" would dissolve into the Hippie Subculture a short time later. Today, we may bump into a hipster, the most recent vestigial subculture to the beatniks who Kerouac represented on his way through Omaha so many years ago.

Part of the culture of the United States is the fact that Americans enjoy the right to worship their gods as they see fit. One of the stranger twists of fate that encumbers Omaha history is that of Congressman Leo Ryan. Like so many US Representative, Ryan had a law degree. He received his degree at Creighton University in Omaha. After graduation he moved to California where he taught school and later ran for office. He was faced with a difficult task when families in San Francisco petitioned him to help them regarding the "People's Temple." His efforts would lead to his death on an airstrip in Guyana. The entire affair would link Omaha with the popular admonition about thinking with your own mind, "Don't drink the Kool-Aid!"

Groupthink and the mania of propaganda can make otherwise lucid people believe in fantastic ideas. When the relatively small Enron swallowed an amenable whale in Northern Natural Gas, it set the investing world on fire. Enron became a gas distribution giant that always seemed to make money and have a rosy outlook. Like an alligator, the ugly and deadly truth lurked beneath murky water. Enron collapsed under the weight of hidden debt and fraud. The ultimate bankruptcy of the company would become the largest failure in American history. The fallout would bring about the most significant change in the way business is governed since the great depression. In the end, Northern Natural Gas would return to where it all started, in America's Hometown, Omaha, Nebraska.

Omaha will continue to write the chapters that make our story so unique. At times it is a saga, at other times it is a thriller, at all times it is interesting. Through the twists and turns that time creates, Omaha has been at the center of American historical events and added our particular essence to American culture. Another story of how Omaha IS America's hometown.

The British are Coming...Omaha to the Rescue?

In 1812, war was imminent with our old relative Great Britain. Like the parent who does not recognize that their child is now an adult, England disregarded the rights and interests of the fledgling United States. England and France were intermittently at war for centuries and this was no exception. As the war intensified with Napoleon's forces, the British sought to blockade all trade with France, even that of neutral parties. England took it one step further and enacted a process called "impressment." Impressment meant that British ships would stop merchant ships and force the sailors to work on British ships. American ships were major targets for this activity at this time and it was appalling to many Americans.

Many in Congress were calling for war and demanding the release of kidnapped Americans. They continued to lament altercations that had brewed between the two countries over the past decade. The English were in a raging war with France and for their part, the British felt like their former colonies were plotting to annex Canada. To satisfy the umbrage, the United States declared war in 1812. There were several problems with the plan.

The United States had become an independent nation in 1776 but it did not have any real government or decision making ability until 1786 with the signing of the Constitution. The US had a very small standing army and a fledgling Navy. Their opponent had the most powerful Navy in the world and a top level army. Firepower was not the only problem facing the United States.

In 1803, the United States found amazing fortune in a purchase Thomas Jefferson made from Napoleon Bonaparte. For about $15 Million, the United States doubled in size. The Louisiana Purchase as it came to be known was fortuitous in peace, but just nine years later in a state of war, the vast increase in borderlands, coastal areas and, Native Americans created far greater challenges to the United States than before.

In 1812, the area of the Louisiana Purchase was mostly undiscovered country for the government of the United States, it hardly knew or understood the Native-Americans that lived there. St. Louis was a well-known city for decades, a center of commerce for the fur trade that dominated European activities in the west. Manuel Lisa a Spanish-American trader travelled from St. Louis up the Missouri River into modern day Nebraska. There he set up a trading post in what is now Northeast Omaha. The outpost would become an important center in the American war effort during the War of 1812 or what some naysayers were calling "Mr. Madison's War."

As the founder of the Missouri Fur Company, Manuel Lisa was in a unique position to gain respect and trust from the tribes on the upper Missouri. The fact that he knew the principle tribes, their leaders, locations and how to communicate made him a natural choice for the government to appoint him the Indian Agent on the Upper Missouri. This made it his responsibility to keep those tribes from becoming allied with the British during the War of 1812.

The US Government had real concerns that the British would try to turn the tribes against the Americans. The British had already advocated for a Native American "buffer zone," on the frontier which would have limited American growth. There were also a number of Americans who still remembered that the French and the English sought Native American support during the French and Indian War.

Manuel Lisa coordinated with the Teton and Yankton Sioux, the Mandan, the Omaha, the Arikara and the Ponca to keep them at peace with the United States. Indeed, in order to promote relations, Lisa, who was married in St. Louis, took a second wife. His second wife was Mitane, the daughter of the principle chief of the Omaha tribe, Big Elk. The union produced children and developed greater clout for Manuel Lisa among the tribes he encountered.

The War of 1812 did not go exceptionally well for the United States. The British had the American Navy bottled up and had effectively blockaded merchant activities out of the United States. The US was going bankrupt fighting the war with very little coming into the coffers. On top of fighting the British, the United States was faced with hostilities from some Native American tribes.

In 1813, war erupted in Southern Georgia with the Creek Indians who the American government hoped to displace. Andrew Jackson was forced to knock down this uprising before moving on to meet the British who were sailing towards one of the most important ports in the United States at the time, New Orleans. The US could ill-afford more conflicts internally as the faced a large British force bearing down on them.

After fighting through the Indians, Jackson made his way to New Orleans and in late 1814 was able to achieve one of the most lopsided victories in history when the outnumbered American soldiers and their pirate allies routed the British. There were no threats from the upper part of the Louisiana Purchase due to the work of Manuel Lisa.

The Battle of New Orleans was supposedly fought after the war had ended. That is not true. What is true that the Treaty of Ghent which was signed December 24th, 1814 and the pivotal battle of New Orleans took place on January 8th, 1815, the Senate did not ratify the treaty until February 17th, 1815.

Omaha had a place in American culture before it was launched as a city. Manuel Lisa, the first American settler in Nebraska was a Spaniard, married to a Native American, and dedicated to keeping the peace with the Indians. His work helped the United States avoid defeat in the War of 1812, all from his small fort in North Omaha.

The Potawatomi Indians probably wished that they lived near Poison Oak! That their tribal lands were teeming with thistle. Instead, French gastronomists found a piece of land on the southwest shore of Lake Michigan, an area covered with wild garlic. For this reason, the area was referred to by one of the first explorers, Robert De LaSalle as Checagou, a disambiguation of an Illini word for "Wild Garlic."

The land had passed though native hands several times into the late 1700's when European power started to take ownership. In 1813 the Potawatomi had ceded much of their land. The leader of the Indians around Chicago was a half-Potawatomi, half-Scottish chief named Billy Caldwell. He built the first real home in Chicago and organized the first Catholic Church. But in 1833, the city wanted to expand and Europeans wanted to flow into the burgeoning metropolis.

For the sake of 200 Europeans then living in the Chicago-area, 2000 Potawatomi Indians were displaced and pushed from the area. But where to send them? Billy Caldwell, or Chief Sauganash as he was known by his people, led them to Northwest Missouri where they were almost instantly sent away. From there, the Potawatomi, many tired and sick were again forced by the government to move north.

The Potawatomi would march into a new semi-permanent home in the area that would become Council Bluffs, IA. By 1837, the Potawatomie had established a settlement in the Loess Hills that bordered the Missouri river valley. A devout Catholic, Billy Caldwell called on the Jesuit faction of the Catholic Church to establish a mission in Council Bluffs. Within a year, Belgian-born Jesuit Priest Pierre-Jean De Smet would found the St. Joseph Mission in an old military Block House near the Indian settlement.

DeSmet brought religion to the Indians of the area, and consecrated the first Catholic Church. The mission also included the first school in the area. The priest and his aides ministered to the Potawatomi and traveled into the wild hinterlands of the Great Plains to find new groups of Indians to which they might proselytize. They returned to Council Bluffs after their missions to find the Potawatomi dwindling as a group. Those who were left were consumed by alcoholism. De Smet continued his efforts until 1841, when the last baptism was registered in mission paperwork. By this time, the original 2000 indians that had come with Billy Caldwell to Council Bluffs had dwindled to a about 50 families.

Caldwell died of cholera that same year and soon after the rest of the Potawatomi dissipated into Kansas and elsewhere. The diaspora of Billy Caldwell's tribe allowed Chicago to expand from a tiny mud flat to a major metropolis. It would not be the last to owe its beginnings to the metro-area. Not long after the Potawatomi left Council Bluffs, a new religious order rolled into Council Bluffs from Nauvoo, Illinois.

The group was led by Brigham Young who had taken over for the founder of the religion. Joseph Smith created the order based on visions he had in the woods near his home near Palmyra, New York. The new religion was promoted as a further testament of Christianity and its adherents were known as the Church of Jesus Christ of Latter Day Saints and colloquially as the Mormons. The church was controversial and was met with a great deal of animosity. This forced Smith and his followers to travel West to what the prophet called "Zion," or the promised land.

The Mormons first travelled to Missouri but were soon driven out. They fled East to Illinois where they attempted to set up a new community, but here too they face persecution.

In 1844, Joseph Smith and his brother Hyrum were being held in the Cathage, Illinois jail after being charged with inciting a riot. A group of men with blackened faces, holding theological disagreements with Smith raided the jail. The brothers tried to fight the intruders but both were killed.

With the death of Smith, it became clear that there was no place for the Mormons in Illinois and it was time to travel to Zion. The people started in spring, slogging across the muddy Iowa, tallgrass prairie. It took them 4 months to reach the relative safety of what would come to be known as "Kanesville," or modern-day Council Bluffs, Iowa.

Soon after arriving in the area, the Mormons requested help from the US Government to continue the move to their Zion in the Great Basin area of the United States. President James K. Polk offered assistance if the Mormons would form a battalion to assist the military against Mexico. The saints complied and raised a Battalion of about 500 men. The 5 companies of Mormon men set out from Council Bluffs and headed southwest. Over the next 6 months, the battalion would complete the longest military march in United States history when they reached different areas of Southern California.

The Battalion built a road from Santa Fe, New Mexico to San Diego, California. This was not only an important development during the Mexican-American War, but it was integral in the Gadsen Purchase years later. Their work in and around San Diego and other parts of Southern California actually secured the area for the United States. The presence of the battalion in the area actually insured the peace in California until the Treaty of Hidalgo was completed.

In all, the Mormon Battalion made secured Alta California as an American state. Their presence in Southern California made sure that San Diego was ceded to the United States after the war and their wagon roads helped to insure emigration to California from the east. With the end of hostilities with Mexico in 1847, the battalion was disbanded and allowed to rejoin the larger community of Mormons who had made their way to the Great Salt Lake.

Many of the Mormon battalion members headed north to an area owned by a Swiss Immigrant, Johann Sutter. It was here in 1848-49 where veterans of the Battalion working for Sutter discovered Gold. The discovery of gold at Sutter's Mill created the California Gold Rush as well as a population boom in Northern California. Most of the new miners would flow through Council Bluffs, Iowa to be outfitted for the cross-country journey. The gold rush ballooned the population and helped created the modern cities of San Francisco and Sacramento.

Battalion veterans returned to the flock in Utah after the Gold rush. Others like Stephen Clark Foster went to Los Angeles and became the first mayor. Others sought out the next opportunity to strike it rich in the mining industry. In 1850 while travelling to the gold fields of California, Mormon pilgrim William Prows became stuck at the base of the Sierra Nevada during heavy snows. To pass the time he and his team panned for gold. The group successfully discovered Gold in the area which brought a new attention to the region by prospectors.

Prospectors continued to work the area intermittently, continuing to draw gold and silver ore from the earth. Finally, in 1857, while working a failed gold claim, the Comstock Lode was discovered in the area. The Comstock Lode was the largest silver strike in the history of the United States and it too brought thousands of people to the area and helped establish the towns that would soon make up the state of Nevada. Mormons moving into the region from Council Bluffs would eventually create dozens of communities in the Western United States including almost all of Utah.

About the time the Comstock Lode started producing silver, serious discussions had begun in the East in regards to a trans-continental railroad. With the controversy of the Kansas-Nebraska Act, Abraham Lincoln was goaded into action to run for President in the newly created Republican Party. Lincoln had just lost a Senate race to Douglas in 1858 but the debates the two shared gave Lincoln national name recognition. In 1859, Abraham Lincoln visited Council Bluffs during a campaign tour. He also took the opportunity survey property deeded to him in Council Bluffs as collateral for legal services.

While in Council Bluffs, railroad engineer and future civil war General Grenville M. Dodge worked and cajoled the future president about benefits of Council Bluffs becoming the Eastern Terminus of the transcontinental railroad if it were built. Lincoln saw this plan as advantageous for himself as it meant an increase in value for his land. So in 1863, during the throes of the Civil War, Lincoln gave the nod to Council Bluffs as the terminus. With the approval of the US Congress preparations for government assistance on the railroad began in earnest.

After fighting in the Civil War, Colonel Grenville M. Dodge was reassigned to battle Indians in the west. In 1864, Dodge ordered a fort to be raised in Southwestern Kansas. Col. Dodge sent out crew with too few provisions and upon completion, the disgusted soldiers named their building, Fort Dodge. By 1871 a city would spring up nearby that would be integral to the history of the west. Dodge City, Kansas was named after General Dodge and helped to create the legends of Bat Masterson and Wyatt Earp.

In 1866, after warring with plains Indians, Grenville Dodge resigned his commission in the US Military in favor of going to work building the railroad. As chief engineer of the railroad, Dodge created the route for the road. The railroad was also grants substantial land as right of way on either side of the rails in order to build towns and cities. One of the first major towns created came when the "support train," could no longer keep up with the builders.

When the construction of the railroad began, a support train followed the builders. The train was filled with materials for makeshift saloons, a variety of prostitutes and sundry other vices meant to be of comfort to the men working on the railroad and to keep them doing their job. The support train was given the moniker, "Hell on Wheels." When the road became too distant for the train to continue back and forth from Omaha each day, a town sprang up to fulfill the need. The first city was called North Platte, Nebraska. North Platte became a major city for Western Nebraska and was important for its roll in WWII.

As the railroad moved into Wyoming, Dodge named a newly platted town after an area Indian tribe. He loved the name, Cheyenne. As the road moved west the company platted another town Laramie, Wyoming. The railroad eventually reached Utah and linked up with the railroad extending east from San Francisco. This would not be the end of the Union Pacific's creation of towns. Dozens of cities throughout the western United States were developed by the railroad or were formed when the railroad came to a terminus.

For his part, Grenville M. Dodge engineered railroads all over the world including the Trans-Siberian Railway. He also consulted on 30 other American railways which had their own railway towns. This led to dozens of others towns throughout the United States being formed. All of which had their beginnings in the Omaha metro-area.

Fake News and Instant Messages: Rosewater, Lincoln and Trump

It wasn't just any war. It was unlike any war ever fought in human history. Never had one army pitted itself against another army to bring freedom to all men. One side believing that its logic and reason absolutely sound that all men should be free, the other believing themselves persecuted by a government. A government that was egregious in their demands especially in regards to the sake of an inferior race.

As the conflict tore at every seam of what was America at the time, life did not stop. People went about their lives, knowing battles raged around their country. They heard reports and read the papers. The papers were fed by the telegraph. Telegraph operators tapped out messages from all over the country like so many Tweets in the modern day.

The telegraph operator could describe troop movements and offer real-time reports about battles. Rather than Pheidippides running to Athens with the results of the Battle of Marathon, people in far-away places could receive the message instantly by Morse code. Abraham Lincoln was enamored with the technology and like Donald Trump over 150 years later, he sent messages prolifically.

At the outset of the Civil War, Ohio born Edward Rosewater was in Stevensen, Alabama in his new profession as a telegraph operator. His role meant that he came across a number of high ranking Confederates including fellow Jew, Judah Benjamin and President of the Confederacy Jefferson Davis. In May of 1861, Rosewater moved north to work at the Nashville Telegraph office but resigned after Nashville fell to the Union in 1862.

Rosewater was fiercely loyal to the Union cause and in April 1862, volunteered for the Union Army. His skills put him in the employ of Generals. By the summer of 1862, Rosewater was attached to General John Pope. Pope led a campaign against Robert E. Lee and was routed at the Second Battle of Bull run when he was outflanked by General James Longstreet. It fell to Edward Rosewater to telegraph the news back to Washington and to decipher the command relieving Pope of his command two weeks later.

Rosewater's skill in dispatching reports from the battlefield at Manassas led to an appointment at the War Department in Washington DC. It was here that Edward Rosewater came in contact with many important figures of the Civil War era. Lincoln was there sending messages to the battlefield, demanding information, demanding action. Rosewater was there when the Union Army finally had an important victory at Antietam. Rosewater was also sending messages to McClellan, prodding him to attack Lee. In fact begging him, only to meet with intransigence. When Lee slipped away, Rosewater sent out the orders to relieve McClellan.

The victory at Antietam gave Lincoln the traction he needed to do what he himself considered the crowning achievement of his life. In September of 1862, Abraham Lincoln crafted the Emancipation Proclamation to be telegraphed to all of the states that were in rebellion. Edward Rosewater tapped out the 719 words that freed 75% of the slaves living in the United States. It was a document that changed history and the entire course of American history.

Perhaps it was the gravity of the event that he participated in, or perhaps the continued stress of the war caused Edward Rosewater to stop and take note of his life. In 1863, Edward

Rosewater left the Army and Washington DC to become the Chief Operator for the Omaha City Telegraph. Omaha in 1863 was a frontier town. To call it a "town" may be overstating its development by that time. Omaha didn't even have a school until September of 1863.

In 1871, Rosewater started the Omaha Bee newspaper. Rosewater had no intention of starting a true newspaper, his interest was in forming public opinion and pushing political subjects he was interests in. The first issue was the Omaha Board of Education, which, through his editorial goading, was enacted in 1871. This was the first of many issues pushed by the Republican newspaper in the years to come.

Edward Rosewater was not a trained journalist nor did he have any experience with publishing a newspaper. The newspaper reflected more about Rosewater's opinion than any real news. As time went on, the paper drifted toward sensationalism and yellow journalism. Articles with elements that went against the editorial position were often filled with sniping comments, criticizing more from passion than with facts. The style which was common of the time created many enemies for Edward Rosewater and resulted in more than one physical altercation.

With the various waves of immigration that entered Omaha, the Omaha Bee was there pontificating on the benefits or detriment each people group had on society. The Bee would express disdain for different ethnicities and excite common discord. This was especially true during the Greek riots in Omaha in 1909.

> "The thing that sticks in the crow of the anti-Greek element is that they work cheap; live even more cheaply. in groups; are careless of many of the little details that Americans set much store by; once in a while are impudent, ignore the restrictions of American law that lay heavily on the true patriot-in short, do not mix, are not good fellows" like the citizens we get from northern Europe, for instance."

Edward Rosewater died in 1906 and was honored in 1910 when the Omaha School Board named a new school after him. His early life and accomplishments of spreading the news of the Emancipation Proclamation helped the Union to win the war and Lincoln to bring the country back together.

Rosewater was part of delivering the news of one of the greatest executive orders in US Government history. He was part of the chain that allowed a president to send out numerous messages of criticism and management, sometimes of ridicule as is seen in this famous reply to Gen. George McClellan after he refused to press Robert E. Lee after the Battle of Anietam.

Lincoln replied to McClellan after the General complained of tired horses. Lincoln replied in an almost bullying manner "about sore-tongued and fatigued [sic] horses," Lincoln demanded to hear from McClellan, "what the horses of your army have done since the battle of Antietam that fatigue anything?" Does this sound like anyone who uses a modern technology to berate his subordinates and others who frustrate him?

Rosewater was part of the best of our history and part of the worst. When he developed his newspaper, he used sensational and yellow style journalism. Stories and opinions meant to move public opinion to his thinking. Often the stories were dubious and apocryphal; something that today may be called "fake news!" From Lincoln to Trump, what is old, becomes new again and of course, Omaha had its invisible hand mixing the pot.

Bongo Drums in Omaha?

Omaha was the scene Daddio and it was one of the subjects of one cool cat who started a whole generation. Jack Kerouac, he was the King of the Beat generation and it all stemmed from the success of his iconoclastic novel, "On the Road." People who got involved with the "Beat" lifestyle were referred to as "Beatnik." The "Beat," generation was a subculture that was interested in Eastern Religions, despised materialism and liked to explore hedonism in all of its forms.

This mentality came in part from the rambling prose of Kerouac's book. A young man misses his friends and annoyed with life in Massachusetts sets out almost spontaneously on a cross country journey. His travels are replete with trials and tribulations and moments where he romanticizes taboos of the day. He bummed rides from people he knew or he hitchhiked. When he could not find a car he would stow away on trains where he could. It was rare when he was not drinking alcohol or smoking cigarettes.

The image he portrayed was one of a carefree life devoid of responsibility. He wrote of characters, his friends and their similar exploits of living a semi-communal lifestyle and describing the exploits of the scandalous. He rode the rails into Council Bluffs, Iowa, dreaming to see Old West settlers heading out in wagons but instead saw, "only cute suburban cottages of one damn kind and another, all laid out in the dismal gray dawn."

Getting across the river he found himself in Omaha where he seemed to have passed through noting what would have definitely been true to form of the day the cattlemen and the packers:

> "Then Omaha, and, by God, the first cowboy I saw, walking along the bleak walls of the wholesale meat warehouses in a ten-gallon hat and Texas boots, looked like any beat character of the brickwall dawns of the East except for the getup. We got off the bus and walked clear up the hill, the long hill formed over the milleniums by the mighty Missouri, alongside of which Omaha is built, and got out to the country and stuck our thumbs out."

Kerouac may have felt at home in Omaha. The way he writes he was traveling through South Omaha. The immigrant, Catholic community of the downtrodden which the "Beat" writers tended to be infatuated with. Kerouac for his part hated to be called, "King of the Beat Writers," he often proclaimed "I'm not a beatnik, I'm a Catholic." Despite his disagreement with the moniker, his work influenced a variety of artists that survived him including Jim Morrison and the Doors, Bob Dylan and Hunter S. Thompson.

Whatever the Beat movement was or is, depending on your perspective, for Kerouac and his circle of contemporaries like Allan Ginsburg and William Burrough's did not seem to be purposefully creating a sub-culture indeed Kerouac explained to a student who asked about the meaning of "On the Road," he explained:

> "Dean and I were embarked on a journey through post-Whitman America to find that America and to find the inherent goodness in American man. It was really a story about 2 Catholic buddies roaming the country in search of God. And we found him."

The Beat movement was eventually swallowed up by the hippy movement in the late 1960's which brought many of the original social activities and interests of the beatniks to the mainstream. In the 1950's for example, marijuana tended to be a drug used by jazz musicians and behind closed doors in hushed tones. Since Kerouac's visit in Denver and San Francisco, both cities are wide open for the drug and the idea of legalization of marijuana pervades in modern society.

Kerouac stopped by Council Bluffs, depressed by its collection of mismatched small homes. He saw no reason to stop and explore the meat metropolis that was Omaha in the early 1950's. Regardless, Jack Kerouac was sober enough to remember us in his rambling, scroll of an autobiography. How could he forget, America's Hometown.

"Don't Drink the Kool-Aid."

"Ask not what your country can do for you but what you can do for your country." This quote is familiar to so many who grew up in the days of Camelot and the coming of age of the baby boomers. So many young people were motivated to devote their time to building America. One man who was a chaperone for the marching band at the high school where he taught heard John Kennedy's inaugural speech was motivated to go above and beyond teaching young people and became a social justice warrior.

Ryan chose to run for elected office and in 1962 was elected Mayor of South San Francisco, CA. Less than a year later he would resign his position to take a seat in the California Assembly. In the assembly he would build a reputation for going above and beyond in benefit of his constituency. He also tended to do things and go places in the execution of his duties that could have put him in real danger.

Perhaps this was learned in college at Creighton University in Omaha. The school was founded on the Jesuit philosophy. This philosophy stresses justice for the underserved and the less fortunate as well as a tendency to take on challenges that no other religious orders would attempt. This devotion has earned them the sobriquet of "God's Marines."

Leo Ryan's sense of social justice influenced what a colleague described as, "experiential legislation." Ryan went undercover as a substitute teacher to learn more about the problems and situations in the neighborhood after the Watts Riots in Los Angeles. Folsom prison had long been criticized by inmates and their families for the treatment they received. To investigate this, Ryan had himself arrested and went undercover as an inmate to investigate the problems in the prison system. Regardless of the issues that faced California, Leo Ryan worked to meet the challenge.

Ryan took his experiential legislative style to Washington DC in 1972 when he was elected to the US House of Representatives. The problems he faced as an Assemblyman were nothing compared to what was coming for him. His willingness to face danger for the benefit of his constituents would continue to be his hallmark and the biggest problem of his life was brewing just as he entered office.

In the early 1970's, Reverend Jim Jones was building a statewide ministry in California. By 1972 he was focusing on Northern California and more specifically San Francisco. Jones used his personal charisma to develop a following in the inner city of San Francisco and his message became especially compelling to African-Americans. Jones used his burgeoning church to become a political power. He compelled his parishioners to volunteer for specific candidates and he told them to vote for the candidates of his choice.

His efforts were specifically notable for the close election of George Moscone as Mayor of San Francisco and for the election of Harvey Milk. These political connections helped him avoid controversy and to build his People's Temple without government scrutiny for a time. This would all change with the execution of his Agriculture Project in the jungles of Guyana.

In 1974 Jones and his inner circle flew to the British Colony of Guyana on the Northeast coast of South America. There they leased a large parcel of land which would become the People's Temple Agricultural Project. In California, he was telling his parishioners to sell their belongings and give it all to the church. The people drawn to his charisma did as he told them to.

The first groups travelled to Guyana to build the settlement. Then in 1977 after some members left the group and sought help for their grievances from the local press, Jones and the rest of the church chose to make a clean split. They all left California and travelled to Guyana en masse.

Family and friends left behind were skeptical of the group and the oleaginous Jim Jones. With reports of abuse from the church trickling out into the media, these families formed a group called "Concerned Relatives." The pleas of this group along with newspaper stories caught the attention of Leo Ryan who pledged to visit the settlement in Guyana to see what was happening. Another one of his "experiential legislative" duties.

What had been happening at the commune in Guyana was the indoctrination of political philosophy being disguised as a religion. Jones had forced his congregation to toil in the infertile soils of Guyana during the day and to study communist thought and theory by night. Many people had grown weary of Jones rhetoric and had lost faith in the future he had preached. For his part Jim Jones began to become constantly paranoid and his health began to suffer. He started to preach more and more about their enemies and how the Temple could very well be besieged by those enemies.

Ryan visited the compound in 1978 and some members of the church surreptitiously asked for his aid in leaving. Others still under the spell of Jim Jones were completely subservient and obedient to the will of the church. One of these people attacked Leo Ryan with the attempt to kill him. Ryan escaped unharmed and left to return his plane. Members of the Jonestown "Red Guard," accompanied them and followed them into the plane where they opened fire on the Congressman and his entourage. Congressman Ryan was tragically killed.

Jim Jones recognized that this was the end and led the congregation to drink poisoned glasses of grape flavored drink mix from a communal barrel. Families drank it, parents gave the poison to their children and in the end over 900 people died that day at Jonestown. This gave rise to the common epithet admonishing, "Don't drink the kool-aid." Meaning do not blindly follow those not looking for your best interests. Some of the members hid in the jungle and survived the ordeal. Jim Jones went to his cabin and shot himself in the head. Until the 9/11 Massacre, this was the largest loss of American life in peacetime.

Leo Ryan's bravery was not forgotten and he was awarded the Congressional Medal of Freedom posthumously. The entire episode remains a troubling enigma, but what remains is the values instilled in Ryan during his life in Omaha, Nebraska of being a man dedicated to others and seeking the betterment of the downtrodden.

The Minnow that Swallowed the Whale

Northern Natural Gas might not be a name that everyone in America knows but it has its place in history. A startup in 1930, just after the markets crashed, driving America into depression. The new company began at a time when natural gas was inexpensive, allowing it to flourish in a difficult economic environment. The market appetite for the cheap fuel allowed the company to expand quickly and more than doubled their size by 1932. Their pipeline and distributorship grew throughout the Midwest allowing them to bring gas to new markets. Like many Nebraska companies, Northern Natural Gas had conservative goals and made cautious acquisitions. This model was successful and by the late 1970's, Northern Natural Gas was the largest natural gas distributor in the world.

With all of the acquisitions and mergers that took place, Northern Natural Gas and its holdings reorganized into a single entity called Internorth. The company continued to grow into the early-1980's and remained a force in gas distribution, marketing and even became a player in the plastics industry. Even with the success Northern Natural Gas and Internorth had achieved, they were moving into the new and dangerous waters of the 1980's corporate atmosphere.

By the mid-1980's there were pirates at Internorth's doorstep. Irwin L. Jacobs a Minneapoolis based corporate raider was buying up stock in Internorth. Jacobs had been successful at buying companies, breaking them up and selling the pieces off. He was so successful in fact that he was nicknamed "Irv the Liquidator." Jacobs is also rumored to be the muse for the Richard Gere's character, Edward Lewis in the film Pretty Woman.

With Jacob's continuing to clamor for control, the executives of Internorth looked for a solution. They could either buy back Jacob's shares at a higher price in order to retain control, this is referred to as "Greenmail," or they could take on a poison pill. The company would engage in a merger, thereby making the company too expensive to take over. In 1985, Internorth acquired Houston Natural Gas for $2.3 Billion to become the poison pill and rid themselves of Irwin Jacobs.

The problem is, Jacobs didn't leave, he still owned a large percentage of the new company's stock. While the company was supposed to have dual headquarters in Omaha and Houston former Houston Natural Gas CEO Kenneth Lay made a move to grab power, get rid of the corporate raider and seal the fate of what would be soon be known as Enron.

With Jacobs lurking, Lay borrowed $400,000,000 from the Employee Stock Ownership Program and paid Jacobs greenmail. The much smaller Houston Natural Gas has succeeded in being the minnow that swallowed the whale in Northern Natural Gas. The loan from the company retirement plan became an every growing problem.

As time went on and the company continued to make moves in the energy industry, their debt issues were never covered. Instead Enron started to and continued to enact creative accounting activities. They essentially hid their problems and accentuated their positives to push their stock prices higher. The debt from the ESOP program that Kenneth Lay created kept growing. The interest kept growing and the problem ever worsened for the Enron team.

Kenneth Lay implemented a system called "mark to market," accounting to continually re-evaluate the value of Enron assets. The problem was that Enron had a number of bad business deals on its books and there was also…that…debt. Enron continued to keep it blue-chip stock prices high through marketing, accounting and illusion. Without solving the problems, they started recording profits from projects they had not realized yet. In short the company became its own large Ponzi scheme.

All of this came to a head in 2001 when Enron's accounting company Arthur Andersen, revealed a variety of accounting irregularities from throughout the 1990's. Enron CEO's knowing the internal rot of the company quietly started selling their stocks. Shockingly they kept promoting that they believed that the value of the stock would increase to $140 even as it continued to plummet. By January 2002, Enron stock which a year before had traded around $90 dollars was worth pennies.

Enron declared bankruptcy and sold off most of its holdings. The breakup they had avoid so many years before finally happened. This time another billionaire came to buy one of the pieces. In July 2002, the Oracle of Omaha, Warren Buffett bought Northern Natural Gas from the carcass of Enron and brought it back home to Omaha. It still owns the largest gas pipeline in the United States.

To repel a corporate raider in Omaha, a series of events created the biggest economic scandal in the history of the United States. Enron changed how we do business. In the end, the minnow couldn't keep the whale down and it swam back o where it was born. Omaha, Nebraska